FACING TERROR

The Government's Response to Contemporary Extremists in America

Jim Rodgers
Tim Kullman

University Press of America
Lanham · New York

To my mother, Rosemary,
who instilled in me a desire to search
and to understand others.
—T.K.

To Ana, my daughter;
Ethel, my paternal grandmother;
Joseph W. Jackson, my maternal grandfather;
and Stuart Miller, my friend.
Their voices have opposed violence and chaos
and supported reason.
—J.R.

Contents

Preface

Years of teaching undergraduate courses concerning politics, social problems, and special topics in the social sciences (including terrorism) have convinced the authors of the value of using historical and analytical approaches to teach and learn about difficult national and international issues. Events leading up to the catastrophic violence at Oklahoma City in April of 1995, and the increased public attention given to militia groups thereafter, convinced us of the need to research and write this text as a means of applying historical social science analysis to the American government's attempt to deal with right-wing extremism. Such extremism had, by the mid-1990s, appeared in a number of acts of political and racial violence throughout the country. The extremism warrants, we believe and we contend, a systematic treatment and description, concise but thorough, accessible to the undergraduate student and citizen observer of American violence alike.

This work begins with an introduction that covers a number of definitions and descriptions of terrorism, including that type carried out on the domestic front by groups and individuals. National and international groups are highlighted and a historic context is provided. In subsequent chapters we explore the history of fear and hate in America and the rise and activity of many hate groups from the period of World War I to the present. Mini case studies of domestic terrorist incidents and hate crimes from the past decade comprise another chapter. An important follow-up to that chapter includes profiles of current group leaders in the militia and related movements. The text then sets forth a historical analysis of government responses to terrorist actions. The conclusion explores current questions and issues regarding domestic terroristic violence and provides suggestions for improving understanding and social/political responses. Helpful aids such as chapter review questions and suggestions for further reading appear at the end of each chapter. A glossary, an extensive bibliography, and an index are also provided to assist the reader.

A number of texts have devoted themselves to international terrorism. Numerous contemporary writers have characterized militia groups from a philosophical or journalistic stance. We hope the reader will be engaged in the study of this critical issue through analysis, discovery, history, introspection, and social science, not preconceptions or hyperbole. We have attempted to build upon the works of others and to expand the effort to understand the development of domestic terrorism as an issue in America through the helpful framework of history and social science.

J.R.
T.K.
2001

Acknowledgments

The authors gratefully acknowledge the support and encouragement of many family members and friends in the course of developing and revising this work. We are also very thankful for the support given to us by the administration and faculty at St. Mary's University in Winona, Minnesota, who continue to sustain us in our scholarly endeavors. The sabbatical awarded to Professor Rodgers for the spring 1999 semester especially helped to facilitate the field observation and research necessary for the completion of this work.

The authors are indebted to Professor James A. Aho of Idaho State University for his inspiration, for his pioneering work in the study of militia groups and other extremists in the contemporary American West, and for making available to Professor Rodgers many of his own research files pertaining to extremist groups in Idaho and Montana.

The authors also would like to thank Alan Virta, Head of Special Collections at the Boise State University Library, Boise, Idaho, and his able staff for their assistance in the research of extremist group hate mail sent to the late U.S. Senator Frank Church (D-Idaho) over many years.

Thanks also to Dr. Rick Foster, chair of the Department of Political Science at Idaho State University, Pocatello, Idaho, and to members of his department for their advice and encouragement and to Ms. Leslie Goddard, Director of the Human Rights Commission, State of Idaho, for her meaningful insights and information.

Thanks to the many citizens who responded to our questions, particularly the several human rights activists and law enforcement professionals who shared their ideas and experiences with us.*

A special thank you to Pat Mertes in Central Services at St. Mary's University for her diligent typing, assistance, and patience, and to Sue Knopf for copyediting, designing, and laying out the book.

* Due to the nature of their work and in accordance with personal requests, the identities of most of those who provided information through conversation or interviews regarding militia and race hate activities have been kept confidential. Summaries of information gleaned from interviews with James A. Aho and Leslie Goddard were used with their expressed permission. Information taken from Tilove, 1998, "The Coming White Minority," *Minneapolis Star Tribune* [Newhouse News], 3 July was used by permission of Newhouse News Service.

CHAPTER I

Introduction to Terrorism

"In most instances, in the course of the variations states undergo, they usually move from order to chaos and then back again from chaos to order."

—Niccoló Machiavelli. 1532.
The History of Florence (Book V, Chapter 1) .

Over the last four decades of the twentieth century, no social problem, no political challenge riveted worldwide public attention and threatened worldwide citizen security as much as terrorism did. Viewed by western industrial democracies in the post-Cold War era as the most important obstacle to international security and stability and seen by many in the developing revolutionary countries as an acceptable means of achieving significant but impeded national aspirations, terrorism rivals economic development and environmental degradation as the chief international concern for the first decade of the twenty-first century.

In the United States, current policies and approaches to terrorism reflect the slow, often uneven response to the changing face of terrorism Americans have been exposed to in recent years. A popular television program of recent vintage is titled *The Profiler*. The program centers around the efforts of a police psychologist to develop accurate "profiles" of suspected murderers by piecing together evidentiary facts from crime scenes, from victims, and from accomplices to the crime. Most Americans and global citizens of the sixties, seventies, and eighties could have provided a profile of the typical terrorist. This profile would have reflected press reports of the European, Middle Eastern, Latin American, and Asian instances of terrorism which dotted the political and social landscape in the contemporary era prior to the collapse of Soviet communism and its surrogates. What is noticeably absent from this earlier picture of terrorism is a profile of a typical North American terrorist. If attempted, such a profile would have conformed to the popular idea of communist-leaning, bomb-throwing anarchists castigated and feared in the period 1900 to1929. Many years have intervened between the last wave of domestic terrorism at the turn of the century and the spate of tragedies that effectively brought terrorism home in the last years of the twentieth century.

The gap in years and in public consciousness about American terrorism is also reflected in a gap in institutional and policy responses to the challenge of terrorism. Our work is a systematic and analytical examination of domestic terrorism in light of recent instances of terrorist activity that haveonce again, after these many decades, focused Americans' attention on terrorism at home. We direct the reader to four primary areas of concern: 1) the sociopolitical milieu within which the American terrorism of the 1990s took place; 2) dramatic events themselves, with attention to the Oklahoma City bombing and bombings over the past decade in Atlanta and the South; 3) the intergovernmental American responses to the recent terrorist actions; and 4) the probable future needs and expectations of social and political institutions in response to terrorism.

Our objective in this work is fundamentally educational. We wish to engage the reader in a dialogue concerning the problem of domestic terrorism. We seek to pose intelligent questions based on research that will stimulate each reader to rethink important issues and develop answers to the terrorist dilemma. We proceed toward our objective and an analysis of the four primary areas of concern by first setting the context for analysis of terrorism with a review of important definitions, terms, and typologies essential to the development of a working knowledge of terrorism.

Definitions

Early definitions of terrorism were associated with developments in the French Revolution. Most specifically, the term drew its negative connotations form the "reign of terror" of March 1793 through July 1794 in France (Laqueur 1987, 11). The British political theorist and statesman, Edmund Burke, caught the mood and the fears of many of the elite of the eighteenth century European monarchies in a phrase descriptive of the French activists: "those hell hounds . . ." (Laqueur).

While there is no catchall definition of terrorism that covers all aspects of the phenomenon adequately[1], we offer these modern attempts at definition. The 1993 edition of the *American Political Dictionary* defines terrorism as "actions undertaken by governments, individuals, or groups using violence or threats of violence for political purposes" (561). The *New Lexicon Webster's Dictionary* sees terrorism as, "the policy of using acts inspiring terror as a method of ruling or of conducting political opposition" (1992, 1021). *Webster's New Collegiate Dictionary* refers to terrorism as "the systematic use of terror especially as a means of coercion" (1965, 991). The *Political Dictionary* further argues that terrorism is directed toward the acquisition or maintenance of power and has recently been associated with Third World movements for autonomy (562). Most recently, writer Irwin Cotler has argued in an article in the journal *Terrorism and Political Violence* (Summer 1998, 1-14) that terrorism is ". . . [an] assault on human rights and human dignity . . . ." From this moral perspective, Cotler advocates that democratic nations begin to think of counter-terrorism as human rights policy (3).

As stated above, no definition is completely comprehensive. However, assembling the elements of the definitions offered here, the authors conclude that terrorism includes some attempt, using violence—or its threat—or manipulation (economic, political and/or social) directed toward leadership groups in society for the purpose of achieving power and control over them[2]. Title 22 of the U.S. Code, Section 2656 F (d) defines terrorism as "premeditated, politically motivated violence perpetrated against noncombatant[3] targets by subnational groups or clandestine agents, usually intended to influence an audience." The government has relied upon this definition for statistical and analytical policy purposes since 1983. Similarly, the FBI relies upon this definition: ". . . the unlawful use of force or violence against persons or property to intimidate or coerce a government, the civilian population or any segment thereof in furtherance of political or social objectives" (*Terrorism in the United States,* 1982-1992, U.S. Department of Justice, Federal Bureau of Investigation [Terrorist Research and Analytical Center, Counter-terrorism Section Intelligence Division] 1993, Washington, D.C., Appendix A, 20 as cited in Riley and Hoffman, *Domestic Terrorism: A National Assessment of State and Local Preparedness* [Rand Corp.] 1995, 3).

Terrorism has at its base a motivation to achieve power, often by those who lack power or the ordinary resources to attain it. Terrorists wish to affect those in leadership, viewed as socio-economic and political elites, by their aggressive acts. As further exploration of the subject will illustrate, however, terrorists groups frequently use violent acts against the seemingly innocent and powerless (e.g., travelers, office workers, pedestrians, commuters) in order to pressure society's elites to give them recognition and acquiesce to their demands.

Of the researchers of terrorism, Walter Laqueur has come closest to bringing into focus the systematic nature of terrorist group activity (1987, 12). That is, Laqueur sees patterns and group purpose that are associated with terrorist organizations. Understanding these organized efforts of unrest and social challenge is critically important. Despite the organized nature of many terrorist activities, all terrorist efforts do not have the same roots. It is, therefore, instructive to sketch out the various kinds of terrorism that have seemed important to the political and social development of the world. What follows are descriptions and brief analyses of four broad types of terrorism: 1) Individualistic; 2) Systematic; 3) Nation-state; and 4) Ideological-spasmodic. The first two types may be inferred from Laqueur's coverage of terrorism; type three is intuitive and has been addressed in numerous works[4]. Type four, ideological-spasmodic, is offered by the authors as an additional category that may help make sense of current terrorist actions in the U.S. that do not fall neatly into the more traditional categories.

Individualistic Terrorism

Individualistic terrorism is exemplified by the violent, often fatalistic, acts of the social/political misfit[5]. Such a person strikes out at a system and culture s/he detests and feels powerless to change by the accepted means or feels that such means themselves, voting for example, have been corrupted beyond salvation. In short, the individualist terrorist adopts the strategy of attack because of the perceived futility and stupidity of pursuing any other avenue of change. While individualist terrorists may share common goals, affiliations, and ideology with others, they are detached from and not directed by the significant social group with which they share aspirations or affinity. In other words, when they commit acts of terror, the strategy and tactics of the affinity group are not manipulating their actions. They follow their own orders and respond to their own internal motivation and choice of tactics in selecting targets and exercising options. Their actions may, indeed, run counter to those on the agenda of the larger group and may serve to defeat that agenda in regard to both timing and alternatives.

A classic American instance of individualistic terrorism is Leon Czolgosz's assassination of President William McKinley at a public reception in Buffalo, New York, on September 6, 1901. The anarchist disciple Czolgosz shot the president several times at point-blank range while McKinley shook hands with many well-wishers. McKinley died eight days later, and the assassin was tried, convicted, and sentenced to death. Czolgosz was executed at the prison in Auburn, New York, on October 29, 1901 (*New Book of Knowledge* 1993, 194). Though sympathetic to the anarchist cause of that period, which accepted the necessity of violence in order to produce sociopolitical change, Czolgosz seems to have followed his own blueprint and not that of a "movement." As an individual, he set out to strike a blow against a corrupt and oppressive state by means of his own choosing.

International instances of individualistic terrorism include the exploits of Auguste Ravachol and Emile Henry in France amidst the bomb-throwing craze of 1892 to 1894 (Laqueur 1987, 18). Ravachol is described by Laqueur as a bandit who would have killed and robbed even if no anarchist movement had existed at the time in France (1987, 18). Anarchists were on the move during the late nineteenth and early twentieth centuries in Europe and the United States. Further, many of the anarchist persuasion had come to accept violence as a rightful means of achieving anarchist goals during the late 1800s. However, Ravachol and Henry seem to have adopted anarchist sympathies, in part at least, to simply further their respective personal criminal goals (Laqueur 1987). They were not acting out the anarchist conspiracy against European elites and aging monarchies, but they were using anarchist propaganda and ideals as an umbrella to cover for their own motives. They were not exactly pure-criminal types, because they sympathized with and manipulated the anarchist cause to serve their own ends and because they used attacks on the political system as a great means of achieving personal success and prominence.

Systematic Terrorism

Systematic terrorism, in contrast to the individualistic brand, denotes an organized movement toward a set of pre-planned goals by the use, in large part, of agreed-upon actions or tactics. Spontaneity of action is replaced by organized pursuit, often ruthless and surprising to the victims and to the ordinary socio-political power structure. Hurt and frightened citizens frequently react to horrendous acts of terrorism as if "madmen," "deranged" and striking out "wildly" for the perceived wrongs they've been done, were the "irrational" perpetrators of terrorism. With the systematic terrorist, nothing could be more erroneous.

Laqueur illustrates the systematic movements devoted to terrorism in his historical accounts of the Russian Narodnaya Volya, 1878 to 1881, and the later Social Revolutionary Party, 1902 to 1907, and their respective attacks on the czars and other Russian elites (1987, 16). In the United States a significant systematic group has been the Ku Klux Klan (KKK). The second Klan (1915-1944) in particular fits Laqueur's notion of a systematic terrorist movement. Indeed, the KKK exhibited a definite structure, plan, purpose, and agreed-upon set of tactics in attempting to intimidate and destroy racial minorities and in their view "purify" the American culture and government. Further, Klan leaders operated as if the Klan were a business, and they were undone in part by the federal government's investigation and successful prosecution of income tax evasion charges (Laqueur 1987, 14).

Internationally, the Japanese Red Army (JRA) conformed to the systematic model. Formed in 1969 during the general international uprising of students opposed to the Vietnam War, the group had strong revolutionary, socialist aims. Three Red Army members participated with the Popular Front for the Liberation of Palestine (PFLP), a kindred organization, in the 1972 attack on Lod airport in Israel that resulted in the killing of twenty-six people. The Japanese group also hijacked a Japanese Airlines DC 8 in Bombay in 1977 and succeeded in securing $6 million in ransom from the Japanese government and freedom for six of its own who were imprisoned (Dobson and Payne 1982, 184). The JRA shifted its organizational headquarters to Lebanon in 1971 and since the seventies has made the politics of the Middle East its focus. JRA is unique in that in 1981 its leader, Fusako Shigenbou sent a newsletter to Japan in which she renounced the use of violence and stressed instead political unity and consolidation as means of enlarging the movement opposed to western imperialism (1982, 185). While they remain committed to struggle against the "imperialists," the JRA seems to no longer view armed struggle as the method to sustain it.

The JRA's ties to the PFLP brings to mind another Middle Eastern terrorist group of more recent vintage and concern. Hizbollah, Islamic Holy War, has operated heavily in southern Lebanon and in Israel itself since 1985, when the Israeli security zone was set up. The havoc created by Hizbollah has threatened to disrupt both Israeli and Palestinian Liberation Organization efforts to secure a regional, lasting peace. More than two hundred Israeli soldiers have died fighting Hizbollah since 1985 ("Israeli Chopper Crash," *Maclean's,* 17 February 1997, 51). Militant religious zeal and the leadership goals of Muslim clerics and their followers have been critical to the strategy and operation of Hizbollah.

The late Claire Sterling catalogued effectively the substantial systematic terror network often managed and/or manipulated by the Soviet KGB during the Cold War era. Arms, training, money, guidelines and techniques were systematically shared by Soviet operatives and European and Middle Eastern terrorist groups (Sterling 1981).

Systematic terrorist groups may thus be seen to exhibit a particular organizational structure, an avowed purpose or plan, a set of agreed-upon tactics directed at achieving the plan, and a committed leadership surrounded by a core group of followers who will usually do the leaders' bidding no matter how dangerous or violent. Systematic terrorists are those the American public has been used to seeing portrayed on television and in film and covered live by broadcast news programs. Since the'70s and '80s the systematic terrorist has fit the popular image of a Middle Eastern radical in guerilla dress, wielding a machine gun or a grenade, committed to *jihad* against the nation of Israel and all her supporters and friends. Unfortunately, recent and current times, as we illustrate below, have often seen terrorist practices of two other types—nation-state and ideological-spasmodic terrorism.

Nation-State Terrorism

Nation-state terrorism is perhaps the oldest type in existence, and a look at examples from the Old Testament supports such a view. Exodus chapter 14 tells how Pharaoh became angry at the flight of the Israelites and organized a great pursuit in hopes of eliminating Israel's right to leave a nation in which they were originally guests and then laborers. It is perhaps instructive that this very early recorded attempt at nation-state terrorism ultimately backfired (Exodus 14:27, 28 King James version) as so often nation-state efforts of terror as political control do. Later on, in the time of the budding nation of Israel, we also see the efforts by an angry and upstaged King Saul to murder and destroy his political rival, David (I Sam. 18-31 King James Version).

In recent years, nations have practiced purposeful terror against their own citizens and against outsiders protesting or opposing their policies, even if nonviolently. South Africa under apartheid; Guatemala from the 1954 CIA-backed coup to the recent surge of democratic forces (1995-96); Argentina under the reign of the Generals (1976, 1982); Chile under the iron fist of General Pinochet; post-revolutionary Iran as dominated by the Ayatollah and his allied mullahs; pre-revolutionary Iran with the Shah's dreaded Savak; the Soviets, particularly in the period from Stalin through Brezhnev (1929-1982); Soviet satellite governments in eastern Europe during the Cold War period; British empire forces in colonial India and Egypt; German, French, and Austrian monarchies versus colonial peoples in the late nineteenth century, particularly in Africa and the Balkans; the United States in its policies and responses to Native American tribes (1820-1890). All of these seem to be legitimate examples of nation-state terrorism.

Indeed, one could argue, based on the historical record, that nation-state terrorism has resulted in great loss of life and that it has been particularly vicious on many fronts. The general nature of state terrorism was typified by the Somoza regime in Nicaragua, among other Latin American dictatorships of the '60s and '70s.

As Frederick Hacker has retold, torture was routinely applied to political prisoners. A variety of sadistic measures including blinding with electric light, near-drowning, and imprisonment in cages next to wild beasts were among the chosen Somoza methods of dealing with political opponents (Hacker 1976, 54).

In the early 1930s, the elder Somoza ordered the assassination of Nicaragua's and, at the time, the United States' chief nemesis in the country, the revolutionary Augusto Sandino (Hacker). Of course, in 1974 Sandino's memory and vision were revived with a vengeance by the Sandinistas, who ultimately waged war in 1978 and toppled the younger Anastasio Somoza Debayle from power. In Nicaragua in the 1980s, the Sandinistas themselves were bitterly opposed by both the Reagan and Bush administrations. These American politicos regarded the Sandinistas as bedfellows with the great Caribbean Marxist, Fidel Castro of Cuba, and with aspiring Marxist revolutionaries in neighboring El Salvador. The Sandinistas were accused repeatedly of human rights abuses of their own (e.g., forced relocation and containment of the native Miskito Indian population; restrictions on free speech and opposition parties; manipulation and control of the press). Free, competitive elections did take place under the auspices of the Sandinista government of Daniel Ortega in 1990, however, resulting in the election of one-time revolutionary, newspaper publisher, and Sandinista critic, Violeta Chamorro. After years of nation-state terrorism and abuse, Nicaragua today seems on a surer path to stable, representative democracy. Even the Sandinistas, who have remained very powerful in the Nicaraguan legislature—the National Assembly—have approached policy-making more pragmatically with an eye toward practical negotiation with Chamorro and her successor, Aléman, and with states within the region.

While nation-state terrorism has abated in overall quantity with the post-Cold War changes in Europe, South Africa, and elsewhere, it is still experienced in some measure by many minority population groups and is a source of trouble. In post-apartheid South Africa, for example, the mixed-race population rioted in the Johannesburg area, angry at unequal setting of rates for rent, water, and electricity as compared to rates set in "black" townships. The ruling government, led by the African National Congress, was the focal point for this reaction and hostility, which produced the greatest unrest since the end of apartheid in 1994 ("Race Riot," *Maclean's,* 17 February 1997, 51).

Further evidence of the persistent evil of nation-state terrorism may be seen in an examination of the U.S. State Department's *Report 2000—Year in Review* (U.S. Department of State [hereafter referred to as "State"], [www.state/gov] Office of Coordinator for Counterterrorism, Washington, D.C.). The report lists the nations of Cuba, Iran, Iraq, Libya, North Korea, Sudan, and Syria as major sponsors of terrorism around the world. Other recent annual reports (e.g., State 1996, 1-2) indicate that while active support of terrorism has declined in Cuba, North Korea, Syria, and even in Sudan (prior to that country's confusing involvement and disputed connection to the bombing of U.S. embassies in Tanzania and Kenya), Iran, Iraq and Libya still promote and support significant international terrorism (State 1996, 2-6).

Despite recent efforts at political reform by President Khatami, Iran continues to support Hizbollah's vendetta of terror against Israel from southern Lebanon; assassinates dissidents outside the country (e.g., Reza Mazlouman, an official of the Shah's government killed in 1996; Irani dissidents located in Turkey in 1996; Kurdish opposition members in Berlin in 1992); provides financial and material support to various groups, such as HAMAS and Islamic Jihad; and tries to destabilize neighboring governments like Turkey by providing a haven for terrorist groups from such countries (State 1996, 2-3).

Iraq, often in the news because of its refusal to cooperate with U.N. inspections of potential sites for biological and chemical weapons, has continued to harass and kill opposition Kurds and members of the dissident Iraqi National Congress (INC). In November 1996 a Jordanian diplomatic courier was killed on the road to Baghdad. A diplomatic pouch containing 250 Jordanian passports remains missing, and no one has ever been identified as responsible for the crime. Like Iran, Iraq also provides a safe base of support for members of the Kurdistan Worker's Party (PKK), which frequently attacks Turkey (State 1996, 3).

Libya turned over for trial two Libyan nationals indicted for the bombing of Pan Am 103 in 1988, one of whom was found guilty by a Scottish tribunal in the Netherlands. However, Libya has been linked to international abductions of Libyan dissidents. Libya continues to provide support for many Palestinian terrorist groups, especially the Abu Nidal Organization (ANO). Indeed, the ANO's headquarters is in Libya, also the residence of the organization's leader, Sabri al-Banna aka Abu Nidal (State 1996, 4).

Nation-state terror is definitely a serious and continuing problem for the international community and a danger to the security interests of the United States government and to many innocent citizens. Other kinds of terrorism have become as unpredictable, threatening, and hard to control as state-sponsored actions.

Spasmodic Terrorism

Joining nation-state terrorism today is a somewhat new menace for the United States, spasmodic terrorism within an ideological context. This kind of terrorism is exemplified by the sporadic, loosely connected or unconnected attacks on cultural and political institutions in America in the 1980s and '90s by right-wing extremist groups. Groups such as militias argue that the U.S. government is controlled by sinister forces and often plots with the U.N. to prepare the way for a full-scale invasion of our country and a takeover of the government altogether (Baradat 1997, 161). The "Queen of Babylon," as the late Vicky Weaver referred to the federal government in correspondence to the U.S. attorney in Boise, Idaho, is guilty of unpardonable "sins" of political corruption and violations of Constitutional government as the militia groups and their kindred groups see it (283). Kindred groups include so-called Christian Patriots and Christian Constitutionalists as well as others.

Professor James Aho has, in his book *The Politics of Righteousness,* illustrated very well the differences between Christian Constitutionalists (e.g., John Birch Society; Posse Comitatus), Identity Christians (e.g., Scriptures for America; the racist Aryan Nations), and Issue-Oriented Patriots (e.g., Eagle Forum; Christian Coalition Association) (see Aho 1990, Table 1.2. 19). Among values held in common, each of Aho's three major groupings share a faith in Jesus as the world's one and only spiritual savior; a belief in shaping the world and the government according to the Bible; and an often zealous belief that a great evil conspiracy has corrupted American politics and society and must be resisted and, perhaps, combated by righteous political action (1990, 16-17).

Differences exist between these Christian Patriots (see Figure 1), particularly with regard to methods and tactics to be used in resist-

FIGURE 1

Extremist Groups: A Typology

The researcher Paul de Armond of the Public Good Project has developed the following typology of right wing groups and others through the Project's web site: **http://nwcitizen.com/publicgood**

1. **Neo-Nazis:** Merged in the 1970s due to influence of Christian Identity Doctrine practice race

2. **Ku Klux Klan:** Practice race hate and militaristic order.

3. **Christian Identity:** Bible-based; very racist; believe that only Anglo-Saxons (Aryans) are true Christians. Extremely anti-Semitic.

4. **Militias:** Right-wing paramilitary organizations either covert or overt in operations. The armed wing of "Christian Patriots." Very active in Michigan, Montana and Texas.

5. **Christian Patriots:** Broad movement. Includes groups as diverse as John Birch Society and Montana Freemen. Began by Identity believers and far-right Mormons in the 1960s. In the 1970s split into racists who supported neo-Nazi/Klan efforts and reactionary Patriots. In the 1980s many Patriots discovered violent race hatred of the Aryan Nations and the Klan. Have embraced property rights groups such as Wise Use and passive protestors such as Constitutionalists.

6. **Constitutionalists:** They reject contemporary American constitutional/legal theory; resist the effects and actions of modern day agencies, courts, and public officials; oppose taxes and federal control over lands [see Figure 2, Barrister's Inn Christian Constitutionalist, on p. ___ for more information]; want a return to original, "organic," God-inspired Constitution, including only the 1787 document plus the first ten amendments; consider the Bible as the basis for all meaningful law.

7. **Wise Use:** A pro-business group. Establishes and uses local "property rights" groups as a political front; incorporates operations of the Building Industry Association and the Loggers Association in Washington State; developed county secession groups. Started by Rev. Sun Myung Moon and Washington libertarian Alan Gottlieb.

8. **Christian Right:** Loose alliance of politically active religious groups. Oppose social programs such as public education, civil liberties, abortion, feminism. Some are virtually in agreement with the race-directed Christian Patriot groups, but most are not. Those who are not use political activity and public relations as their primary weapons as well as boycotts of offensive institutions like the public schools.

Adapted from Armond, "Putting the Far Right into Perspective," *Public Good Project,* Internet, 1997 (accessed June 1999), 2-5.

ing and fighting the evils of this corrupt nation. Posse members believe in and have carried out direct threats and actions against legal authorities (Aho 1990, 25, 46). John Birchers prefer to wage their "wars" through pamphlets, books, seminars, speeches, and public relations. Christian Constitutionalists often litigate against different levels of government and argue for a return to the basic tenets of the literal U.S. Constitution of 1787. They tend to recognize only the office of county sheriff as a duly constituted government office.

In Idaho and the mountain West many Christian Constitutionalists were raised as Mormons. Hence, they tend to be pro-rather than anti-Jewish (unlike Christian Identity and Aryan Nations adherents). They are inclined to choose decidedly nonviolent methods of defending, as they see it, lawful Constitutional government (Professor James Aho interview, 28 April 1999, Idaho State University, Pocatello, Idaho). (See also the summary of a conversation with a Christian Constitutionalist in the Boise, Idaho, area in Figure 2.)

Likewise, the Eagle Forum, Christian Coalition and Scriptures for America go after moral and political evils through traditionally acceptable political means, such as lobbying, writing, and public relations. The Aryan Nations (note, for instance, the renegade offspring, The Order) has been continually associated with glorifying and promoting violence through its annual Aryan World Congress (see Aho 1990, Table 1.1.8-9).

Right-wing groups are now many and varied. Militias, such as those in Michigan, Ohio, and Pennsylvania, are able to communicate with one another through shortwave radio (Baradat 1997, 161). White supremist groups, who share many ideas and objectives with the militias, get their message out to the dysfunctional and dislocated in society through often sophisticated use of electronic and print media, as Baradat has recounted in his description of Tom Metzger, the California founder of the White Aryan Resistance (WAR) (1997, 284). Though these extreme groups possess organization, structure, and a rambling racist ideology, they fall under our heading of ideological-spasmodic groups because of the way in which they carry out their tactics in opposition to established institutions. Put simply, these groups attack in "spasms" and often in reaction to events they view as evidence of governmental evil. Hence, Rodney King's situation and the subsequent federal civil

FIGURE 2

Barrister's Inn Christian Constitutionalist

A person not wishing to be identified and associated with the so-called Barrister's Inn Constitutionalist group of the Boise, Idaho, area briefly spoke with one of the authors in a telephone interview on May 3, 1999. As Professor James Aho's files at Idaho State University in Pocatello, Idaho, indicate, public letters by the Barrister's Inn group in previous years indicate the following philosophy of the Constitutionalist group: [they are] concerned about bureaucratic regulations, excessive police powers, the loss of a free market system, income taxes, social security, property taxes, foreclosure, dishonest money, and the locking up of public lands. "We consider ourselves Free and Natural Citizens, to whom all of the Common Law Rights under the Constitution of the U.S. apply. However, in order to live in freedom, we have to become students of the law." The statements go on to suggest that citizens can be taught how to defend themselves against unreasonable government action in court, according to time-honored principles—nothing new. People are urged to defend their own interests and to avoid using attorneys.

In the May 3, 1999, conversation the gentleman affiliated with the so-called Barrister's group indicated that he and others simply stood ready to teach and to disseminate materials on how to be trained in the law. If contacted they send out materials. There is no proselytizing, according to this "barrister." "Anyone can be a barrister who is trained in the law," he said. No use of Internet and no phone solicitation take place. His activity amounts to "Serving the Lord daily." He does not grant any detailed interviews, because he feels that he and the group have been misrepresented by post-interview reports in the past. Thus, the Barrister's Inn Constitutionalists reflect a rather passive, educational approach to political/legal issues. They operate much like a correspondence school. You write or call the number on their brochures and for a fee they will send you material ranging from a video law course, to sample motions and briefs, to a complete winning felony case, to information on the history and development of civil and criminal law. (Of note, the Barrister's group accepts only cash, U.S. postal money orders, or gold/silver as payment).

rights convictions of his police assailants prompted the Fourth Reich Skinheads to plot to ignite a race war by killing King and bombing a noted black church in Los Angeles. Fortunately, this plot was foiled by the arrest of the perpetrators (Baradat 1997, 285). The ATF's (Bureau of Alcohol, Tobacco and Firearms) handling of the Waco incident of 1993 and the FBI's (Federal Bureau of Investigation) actions against the Weaver family at Ruby Ridge, Idaho in 1992 created the outrage and climate of hate which may well have produced the tragic bombing of the federal building in Oklahoma City in 1995. Enmity toward media, exacerbated by the racist belief of Jewish control of broadcasting, led to the murder of a Jewish talk-radio host in Denver in 1984 by members of The Order, affiliated with the Church of Jesus Christ Christian and its political arm, The Aryan Nations (Baradat 1997, 285). The Montana Freemen barricaded their farm house in response to government efforts to try to collect back taxes. In each of these examples, the terrorist act or threat was or seems to have been a spasmodic reaction to a triggering event or set of events. No prearranged, systematic plan seems to exist for a proactive commitment to terror. Rather, the right-wing groups emphasized cross-group communication; public relations; convoluted, conspiratorial ideology; preparation for the coming "Armageddon" with the "Queen of Babylon;" and a heightened state of military readiness, anger, tension, even paranoia. Once unpopular, questionable, or sloppy governmental or institutional actions are digested in this abdomen of hate and fear, spasms of violence and terror are almost sure to emerge in one location or another.

It is the spontaneous use of tactics and terrorist action, the spasmodic nature, if you will, of the American extremist groups that makes social and political responses difficult to fashion and implement effectively. In short, though society has been made well aware of many of the beliefs and intentions of these groups, we still do not have an adequate guide to their respective reaction plans or targets, if they have even decided upon any. Mainly, what we have is the stated purpose of the militias and others to defend against the coming apocalyptic invasion or intrusion and the destruction of individual liberties that they believe will be attempted by the federal government and its sinister international allies.

We would do well, however, to remember the admonition of terrorist analyst Bruce Hoffman of the RAND Institute, who argues that radical racist and militia groups have moved beyond mere tax protesting or resisting. These groups cloak their racism in religious doctrines, using scripture to justify the development of armed resistance to government authorities (1999, 18).

The remainder of this work is devoted to four topics: 1) an examination of the social and political conditions that may provide a more inviting arena for the spasmodic terrorists to operate in; 2) an analysis of recent actors and actions connected to right-wing extremism and terrorism; 3) an evaluation of American institutional responses to terrorism; and 4) arguments for the need of more effective means of dealing with ideological-spasmodic terrorism and the social changes and supports that will be necessary to make such policy changes.

We begin with a look at the social and political forces that have helped to form in contemporary American culture.

Notes

1. Laqueur indicates in his work the many varieties of terrorism, but focuses primarily on what he calls "systematic terrorism."

2. Of interest here is the way in which definitions of terrorism parallel the definition of "evil" as applied by noted psychiatrist M. Scott Peck in *The Road Less Traveled* (1978, 279) and *People of the Lie* (1998, 74). That definition, developed by Peck after numerous significant psychoanalytic sessions with those who have perpetrated evil, goes as follows: evil is seen as "the exercise of political power—that is, the imposition of one's will upon others by overt or covert coercion—in order to avoid . . . spiritual growth." To the skeptic the authors would simply suggest that the victims of terrorism (e.g., the World Trade Center or Oklahoma City bombings) would have no trouble equating what was done to them as "evil."

3. According to the report *1996 Patterns of Global Terrorism,* Introduction, page 4 by the U.S. Department of State, "noncombatant" includes, in addition to civilians, military personnel who at the time of the incident are unarmed and/or not on duty.

4. See, for example, Cindy Combs in *Terrorism in the Twenty-First Century* (1997) chapter five for a survey of contemporary state terrorist actions.

5. Misfit is a term used by Eric Hoffer in *The True Believer* (1951). Hoffer's misfits are of two types: *temporary* (those who have not yet found their place in society but usually will) and *permanent* (those whose lack of talent or existence of mental or physical defect prevents them from doing the one thing they crave to do). Committed terrorists would seem to be drawn, in part, from Hoffer's permanent misfit type.

Chapter Discussion Questions

1. Identify and briefly explain your own definition of terrorism. In what way is your definition different from those mentioned in this chapter? In what way is it the same?

2. Discuss the philosophy and attitude of Christian Constitutionalists in America.

3. Identify the following:

   a. Japanese Red Army (JRA)

   b. Hizbollah

   c. White Aryan Resistance

Suggestions for Further Reading

Aho, James A. 1990. *The Politics of Righteousness.* Seattle: University of Washington Press.

Armond, Paul de. 1997. "Putting the Far Right into Perspective." *Public Good Project,* Internet (accessed 1 June 1999).

Combs, Cindy C. 1997. *Terrorism in the Twenty-First Century.* Upper Saddle River, NJ: Prentice Hall.

Laqueur, Walter. 1987. *The Age of Terrorism.* Boston: Little, Brown and Company.

CHAPTER II

Fear and Hate in America

*"Access to the Godhead can also convince men and
women to take issue with the powerful, to denounce the
princes of this world as heretics, sinners or oppressors."*
—Elizabeth Janeway. 1981.
Powers of the Weak. New York: Knopf, 132.

Richard Hofstadter has used the term "paranoid style" to describe
extremists throughout American political history. The "paranoid
style" represents a particular "world view" about politics that the
extremists come to as a result of their personal and cultural journey
in life. The paranoid extremist tends to view his/her political agenda
as urgent. S/he sees the necessity of violence and even revolution
against the political establishment, which is perpetrating a barrage
of unhealthy, unconstitutional, and un-American forces and values (Hofstadter 1996). These forces and values often originate, in
the minds of the politically paranoid, in an international conspiracy
—started, usually, by the corrupt agents of the United Nations.

Violence Is Necessary for Salvation

Liberal race relations, immigration, declining Christian influences, corrupt political institutions—such as the IRS—and other
degrading elements in society (as the politically paranoid would see
the development of culture in America) represent the "wrongs" in

society that true patriots must oppose and defeat. True patriots must show no regard for mercy or compassion as they oppose these cultural forces. No quarter must be asked or given in the critical war for America's future—for America's soul. In such a "holy war," reminiscent of the Jihad of Islamic radicals such as HAMAS in their running battle with Israel, there really are no "innocents" in the world view of patriots of the paranoid position. People must be either with the patriot cause or against it. Tactics used by the paranoid patriot may be justified by cultural, political, and spiritual salvation, which can be achieved only by the utter defeat of the corrupt forces mentioned above. Therefore, assassinations, bombings, counterfeiting, manipulation, threats, and robberies—even at the expense of the endangerment or killing of children—are all justified for those engaged in this patriotic life-or-death struggle.

Christopher Dobson and Ronald Payne indicate that terrorists ". . . have all come under the influence of those political thinkers who preach that violence is essential to make the world a better place for the masses" (1982, 18). Many paranoid patriots, then, have a common philosophical basis. They have rallied around the notion that violence is necessary and, indeed, is nationally purifying (see William Pierce's novel *The Turner Diaries* 1985, for example). Pierce's novel has served as something of a Bible for radical militia activists, including Timothy McVeigh.

Pierce, as director of the National Alliance, described his view of American politics over the Internet in 1995 just after the Oklahoma City bombing (Pierce 1995). He argued that the Murrah Building calamity occurred, as did the Waco, Texas, debacle, as a result of corrupt, conspiratorial government policies. The "crimes" of the government and the politicians, Jewish lobbies, career women, homosexuals, and the like have been foisted upon America. As in Pierce's fictional race war fought by Earl Turner and others, the conflict against the conspiratorial criminal forces of government stooges and their puppet-masters at home and abroad is urgent and inevitable and will be fought by extreme measures.

Hatred for Outsiders Brings Extremists Together

The type of extremism described by Hofstadter and Dobson and Payne and exemplified by the writings of William Pierce has at its base a significant quotient of hatred for those outside the patriots' pure, acceptable American circle. As Eric Hoffer has pointed out, hatred is one of the strongest of all politically unifying agents. "Mass movements," writes Hoffer, "can rise and spread without belief in God, but never without a belief in a devil" (1951, 86). Sharing a common hatred draws even different types of people together; gives them a sense of kinship; and weakens any individualistic tendencies to question, analyze, or resist the hatred (Hoffer 1951, 86-87). Passionate hatred can provide meaning and purpose to those dull of mind or spirit (Hoffer 1951, 92). Hatred, moreover, is often born of genuine, repressed self-contempt. Unreasonable hatreds emanate from an effort to avoid having to face our own inadequacies (Hoffer 1951, 88)—our own contributions to the so-called political and social ills of America. Feelings of superiority, Hoffer argues, do not create hateful contempt. Rather, deep-seated, unreasoned contempt comes from a sense of marginality, inadequacy, and helplessness.

Wronged by one group or one set of circumstances, some turn their vile reaction onto an unrelated group or circumstance (e.g., poor whites in the South, exploited by the Conservative Aristocrats, join the Klan and lynch poor blacks who are similarly exploited) (Hoffer 1987, 88-89). To wrong the hated is to seek justification and justice; indeed, it is to seek salvation for marginal existence. The "depraved creatures" harmed or destroyed are not pitied, as Hoffer sees it, because they are deemed to deserve every punishment, even extermination (1951, 89). They are the damned and must be treated as such.

Extremists Challenge Authority

That many in the aggressive militia movement in the U.S. exhibit the kind of hate described so clearly by Hoffer is not to be doubted. Such hatred was manifest in the Oklahoma City bombing, and utter contempt for others was shown by former Idaho Militia leader Samuel Sherwood on March 2 and 10, 1995, when he told Idaho's lieutenant governor and the press that a civil war could be coming and that some Idaho lawmakers might betray Idaho, aligning themselves with Washington, D.C., and hence might need to be shot. Sherwood emphatically indicated the necessity of eliminating those who would be foolish enough to choose the "wrong" side in the militia's coming conflict (Lambert and Yurman 1995).

Sherwood's comments should also be understood in the context of apocalypse, ideological fear, and hatred that has periodically been voiced, with serious and significant consequences, in

American history. The coming war; Armageddon; the separation of sheep and goats; the ruthlessness of a holy, though physical, combat—all are themes that have been played and replayed by the unheavenly chorus of ideological extremists in the political and social conflict of our nation.

Confrontational tactics are not limited to militia types. The defendants in the Montana Freemen trial expressed similar hateful and confrontational opinions toward the court. Five of the Freemen were found guilty by a jury of crimes related to armed robbery, illegal firearms possession, and submitting false documents to the IRS on Tuesday March 31, 1998. Their charges stemmed from an eighty-one-day anti-government standoff in 1996 at a ranch referred to as "Justus Township" near Jordan, Montana ("Five Freemen Convicted" *Reuters,* 1 April 1998).

Four of the five convicted men repeatedly disrupted their early judicial proceedings by yelling threats and obscene insults. Judge Coughenour ordered Jon B. Nelson, Steven Hance, James Hance, and John Hance removed after they tore up their court name tags, asserting that the court had no jurisdiction over them. Barred from court, these defendants watched the proceedings on closed-circuit TV. A fifth Freeman, Elwin Ward, was acquitted of any crimes associated with the original standoff, but was convicted of trying to pass a phony Freeman "check" to pay his federal taxes. Another Freeman, Edwin Clark, whose foreclosed ranch served as "Justus Township," was acquitted on all charges (*Reuters,* 1 April 1998).

The four aggressive defendants consistently adhered to their philosophy of challenging the authority and jurisdiction of the federal government throughout their confrontation and prosecution. Their distrust and hatred of political authorities was repeatedly made evident. They knew of no compromise with the "devil"— the national government.

The antipathy toward the U.S. government shown by the five convicted Freemen of Montana is indicative of the attitude expressed by many throughout American history who have blamed challenges, problems, and threats to so-called civilized society on a particular demon-like group or a corrupt leader or Antichrist. The learned and dynamic Puritan preachers Cotton Mather and Jonathan Edwards both judged the Native Americans of New England to be the devil's children. Robert Fuller describes the views of the preachers in this regard and also how they accepted the prominent Protestant axiom of their day that the Pope was the Antichrist (1996, 47). Other leaders in colonial New England saw the "image of the Beast" (Satan) in the form of the Anglican Church, in Moslems, and in other assorted "devils," including those who supposedly practiced witchcraft (Fuller 1996, 52-61). Down through history, from the era of the American Revolution to the onset of World War I, alternative demons were, for many paranoid groups in our country, Great Britain, deists, non-Anglo foreigners, Catholics, Jews, Mormons, socialists, and others (Fuller 1996, 74-107).

Inherent in the ideologies and actions of radical right extremists in history are anti-Semitic, anti-Catholic, anti-Black, anti-government and anti-immigrant sentiments. The speed and direction of social change leaves certain segments of the population feeling vulnerable and unrepresented. Because no social movement exists in a vacuum, we will find within every radical right movement economic, social, and political events that galvanize emotional fears into action.

Abcarian and Stanage Identify
Radical Right Characteristics

A comprehensive review of contemporary radical right literature by Gilbert Abcarian and Sherman Stanage (1965) provides an excellent model from which to analyze radical right writings. They identify nine characteristics that consistently appear in virtually all radical right publications and communications, even those previous to their contemporary analysis. We will frequently refer to these characteristics as they arise throughout our historical examination of radical right extremist movements in the United States from the end of World War I to the present day militia and domestic terrorist actions. In addition to the Abcarian/Stanage model, we will use the socio-historical analyses provided by Seymour Martin Lipset and Earl Raab (1970) and Richard Hofstadter (1996) to assist us in better understanding the nature and external factors that trigger twentieth century radical right-wing extremist movements in the United States.

The Abcarian/Stanage model was developed by sampling rightist literature from the late 1950s and the early 1960s. Publications sampled include, but are not limited to, works of the American

Coalition of Patriotic Societies, the American Security Council, the John Birch Society, the Manion Forum, Liberty Lobby, the Minutemen, the Christian Anti-Communism Crusade, and the Circuit Riders (Abcarian and Stanage 1965, 776).

Abcarian and Stanage identified six characteristics that pertain to ideology and three that reflect a particular political style.

The six related to ideology are:

1) *Individualism*—As one of the cornerstones of democracy, individualism is contrasted with all forms of collectivism. Robert Welch, the founder of the John Birch Society, has stated that "collectivism is a European cancer that has spawned governmental centralization that has resulted in massive bureaucracy, erosion of individual freedom and initiative, subversion of the federal system, and violation of the economic laws of man and nature" (Abcarian and Stanage 1965, 779).

2) *Republicanism*—Much of radical right thinking centers on the distrust of democracy, because one of democracy's central themes is equality. In the words of a John Birch Society sticker, "This is a Republic, not a democracy—Let's keep it that way!" (Abcarian and Stanage 1965, 780). Henry Ford, the noted industrialist, anti-Semite, and one-time potential presidential candidate, indicated his contempt for the democratic process when he stated that the only way he would serve would be under special extralegal circumstances. His true feelings become apparent in the following statement, "There might be a war or some crisis of that sort in which legalism and constitutionalism and all that wouldn't figure, and the nation wanted some person who could do things and do them quickly" (Lipset and Raab 1970, 138). Right-wing fear and hatred of immigrants, Blacks, Jews, and Catholics leads rightist thinkers to believe that only a select elite is qualified to govern the masses. It is a curious contradiction that many radical right thinkers have a distrust of government elites but propose their own elitist framework.

A parallel development that supports Republicanism is the racist doctrine of the eugenics movement. If inequality is part of National Law, then it follows that races aren't of equal ability, racial inferiority is a part of nature, and only those of Nordic heritage are fit to govern. Racial purity was a concern of many of the early radical right nativists, and the work of Madison Grant in the 1920s reflects the Anglo-Saxon concerns of racial supremacy. Grant's emotionally charged racial philosophy was quite popular among the Protestant upper class, since it reflected a concern over immigrant growth and the fear of the destructive process of "mongrelization," or race mixing (Higham 1977, 272).

3) *Fundamentalism*—Incorporating both secular and biblical truths, fundamentalism calls for Americans to return to "Americanism" and "eternal truths" (Abcarian and Stanage 1965, 780). The sense that the United States is adrift in an abyss of evil influences that threaten the future of our children and our nation is one of the primary themes of rightist thought. Many Christian fundamentalists, therefore, yearn for a restoration of that kind of God-fearing republic they believe was created by the founding generation of American leaders and has since been corrupted by deviant behaviors and disobedience of God's will, as seen in the Christian Bible.

4) *Purification*—Betrayal and conspiracy are central to the radical right's tenets. A purging of these conspiratorial forces is critical to the survival of the nation. "It is urgently necessary to expose the hydra-headed conspiracy that infests government, churches, educational institutions, and the mass media of communication. Purification is an urgent patriotic duty" (Abcarian and Stanage 1965, 781).

5) *Restoration*—America has lost the "Golden Age" it once had. With the United States' involvement in World War I, other "foreign entanglements," and the rapidly changing political and economic landscape,our quest for isolationism is gone forever. Continued pleas to restore America's past greatness litter the rightist literature. In the words of Ronald Reagan, ". . . in this land occurred the only true revolution in man's history. . . . it must be fought for, protected, and handed on . . . or one day we will spend our sunset years telling our children and our children's children what it was once like in the United States when men were free" (Abcarian and Stanage 1965, 782).

6) *Unilateralism*—Because of foreign influence in the highest echelons of government and the failure of public officials to protect the interests and moral values of our nation, rightists reject all forms of participation into the League of Nations, the United Nations and the North Atlantic Treaty Organization (NATO) (Abcarian and Stanage

1965, 782). Current domestic militias express unilateralism by describing virtually all government activity as part of a massive "New World Order" conspiracy—a plot of some veiled international government poised to take over the world.

The three characteristics that pertain to the political style of the radical right are:

7) *Telescoping*—Compressing categories that are usually considered unique or distinct. Senator Strom Thurmond's belief that "communism is fundamentally socialism" reflects this practice (Abcarian and Stanage 1965, 783). In the "Red Scare" of 1919-1920, all forms of socialism and unionism were considered bolshevism, regardless of the great differences among these political philosophies.

The Socialist Party in America, under the leadership of Eugene Debs and Victor Berger, was opposed to violence as a form of political expression. They believed in reforming the system through legal pressures, which differed greatly from the Bolsheviks' philosophy of universal proletarian revolution and the destruction of the capitalist system (Murray 1964, 25, 33).

8) *Reductionism*—The radical right credo reduces all social problems to their most basic form. Complex patterns of economic discord, shifting demographics, and political discontinuity are reduced to single sources that can be identified and retaliated against with a moralistic and highly charged emotional response. The reactionary Phyllis Schlafly states, "Civilization progresses, freedom is won, and problems are solved because we have wonderful people who think up simple solutions" (Lipset and Raab 1970, 7). Lipset remarks that this reflects "historical simplism," and it is "the ascription of simple and singular causes to complex human events which evokes the image of every historical moment as virginal" (1970, 8). Once simplification has occurred, polarization is enacted: left wing and right wing become evil and good, and an "intolerance of cleavage" becomes concrete (Lipset and Raab 1970, 17).

9) *Protest through Direct Action*—Action programs are a popular way for right-wing organizations to motivate adherents. Direct action is an emotional impulse, not an intellectual one. Anti-intellectualism is closely aligned with anti-elitism, and is seen as a tool to use against the enemy. Intellectuals are seen as manipulators

of the masses (Lipset and Raab 1970, 16). Direct action is seen as a tool of the "plain people" in contrast to the "intellectuals." For example, during the Red Scare in 1919, patriotic societies such as the National Security League, the American Defense Society, and the National Civic Federation sprang up to combat the coming "Red Peril." They declared themselves "public agents" in the fight against "Red Radicalism" (Murray 1964, 84-85). The American Legion was also founded in 1919 by veterans of World War I to "uphold and defend the Constitution of the United States of America," and "Leave the Reds to the Legion," became a common phrase (Murray 1964, 87-88). Due to the disturbing changes in the social, economic, and political landscape of the post-World War I years, the Ku Klux Klan also had a rebirth, (Murray 1964, 91).

Britism Israelism Emerges after World War I

During the World War I era, the fundamentalist doctrine of British Israelism also began to have a significant impact within American religious culture. British Israelism is a nonmainstream theology that represents a wedding of biblical prophecy and secular pseudo-history. It is the theological foundation for today's Christian Identity religion, which has influenced many in the contemporary anti-government movement (see the profile of Pete Peters in Chapter IV). The origins of British Israelism may be found in the works of the Scot John Wilson, in religious writings of the 1940s, and in writings of the Canadian "psychic" Richard Brothers in the late 1780s.

Essentially, the British Israelites hold that the ten so-called lost tribes of the ancient Kingdom of Israel were carried into Assyrian captivity in 721 B.C. as described in II Kings 17. Then the tribes found their way to freedom, and with the assistance of the prophet Jeremiah, among others, made the journey to northern Europe and also to the British Isles (Melton 1978, 446-447). The tribes of Ephraim and Manasseh, inheritors of God's blessings through their father Joseph of Egypt, represent Britain and the United States, respectively. Racist tendencies permeated the notions of the British Israelites as they came to associate God's grace and power with Anglo-Saxon people and God's punishment with people of color. British Israelism reflects the nineteenth- and twentieth-century religious impulses that fueled British imperialism and American nationalism. Two important writers in the British Israelism movement in the U.S. at the turn of the century were M. M. Eshelman, who wrote *Two Sticks* in 1887 and J. H. Allen, author of the still-influential *Judah's Sceptre and Joseph's Birthright* of 1902. Contemporary advocates of British Israelism have included Herbert and Garner Ted Armstrong of the Worldwide Church of God and, recently, the more extreme Pete Peters of LaPorte, Colorado, whose character sketch appears in a later chapter of this book (Melton 1978, 447-448). For thinkers like Pastor Peters, Anglo-Saxon Protestant America is the true and blessed America. Those outside the Anglo-Saxon realm are in various states of degradation.

Protestant Fundamentalism
Demonizes National and International Institutions

The rise of Protestant fundamentalism in the late nineteenth century also seems to have been associated with the demonizing of national and international political institutions. As Fuller recounts, fundamentalists know the essential character of the two beasts of *Revelation*: the tyrannical dictator and the false prophet. Premillennial fundamentalist scholars have been quick to point out the Antichrist nature of institutions such as the League of Nations and, especially, its successor, the United Nations (1996, 160). In *Fundamentalism and American Culture,* the theological writer George M. Marsden points out that prior to World War I, fundamentalist preachers and authors made only scattered references to political evils and political conspiracy theories (1980, 208). After World War I, the fundamentalists began to see evidence that Satan was attacking Protestant America on all fronts (Marsden 1980, 211). Darwinism and humanism taking hold in the public schools; the rise and strengthening of revolutionary communism; the postwar publication of the *Protocols of the Elders of Zion,* with its fictitious account of an international Jewish conspiracy; efforts at promoting a one-world government; these events all were interpreted through the lens of insecurity and came to be seen as supports for the belief that the forces of "the Beast" were everywhere on the march. Often, as in the Roosevelt programs of the 1930s, the ideals of the evil forces seemed, to fundamentalist extremists, to be encouraged and supported by the policies of the federal government. It is in this age, particularly in the late 1920s and throughout the 1930s (Marsden 1980), that conspiracy theories become more prominent in American churches. The government in Washington began to resemble, for many, a dupe at best and a co-conspirator at worst in the worldwide plan to undermine and destroy Christian values and Constitutional government in the U.S.

Paranoid Thinkers Identify Conspiracies

Richard Hofstadter's analysis of paranoid thinking begins by focusing on conspiracy as *the* motivational force in historical events. There is no denying that conspiracies do exist in history, but fundamentalists feel that "history is a conspiracy, set in motion by demonic forces of almost transcendent power, and what is felt to be needed to defeat it are not the usual methods of political give and take, but an all-out crusade" (Hofstadter 1996, 29). The believer in the paranoid mind-set often sees the world through an apocalyptic lens in which time plays a central factor. In the words of Robert Welch, the founder of the John Birch Society, "Time is running out. Evidence is piling up on many sides and from many sources that October 1952 is the fatal month when Stalin will attack" (Hofstadter 1996, 30).

The apocalyptic paranoid position encompasses feelings of pessimism and militancy with no possibility of mediation or compromise. The opposition is reduced to an absolute evil that must be fought to the finish. The usual rules of politics don't apply because "very often the enemy is held to possess some especially effective source of power: he controls the press; he directs the public mind through 'managed news'; he has unlimited funds; he has a new secret for influencing the mind (brainwashing); he has a special technique for seduction (the Catholic confessional); he is gaining a stranglehold on the educational system" (Hofstadter 1996, 32).

The irony in paranoid thinking is that to successfully combat the evil, the paranoid thinker must adopt his opponents' techniques, and through that adoption, he compliments his opponent. Barry Goldwater once stated, "I would suggest that we analyze and copy the strategy of the enemy; theirs has worked and ours has not" (Hofstadter 1996, 33).

Once the paranoid style takes hold, the believer strives to prove that the "unbelievable" is the only thing to be believed. To achieve this, believers start with defensible assumptions and a careful accumulation of facts, or what appear to be facts, and marshal these facts toward an overwhelming "proof" of the particular conspiracy they wish to establish (Hofstadter 1996, 36).

The paranoid style has existed throughout United States history and continues to be a force today. Certain religious beliefs seem to buttress the development of the "paranoid style" in political and social thought.

As Fuller has aptly pointed out, fundamentalists alternately saw the League of Nations and then the Italian dictator Mussolini as the Antichrist, out to gain world domination toward evil ends through duplicity and ruthless power. Separatism and a narrow cultural framework were and are essential to the outlook of many fundamentalists. They seem to see modernity as an innate threat to a decent, Christian way of life. After World War II, the United Nations assumed the mantle of the Antichrist as the organization embraced many of the world's cultures. Such an embrace was evidence of intrinsic corruption, in the opinion of the pre millennialist fundamentalist zealots (1996, 162).

Extremism Grows in Displaced Groups

Amid the turmoil of rapid social, economic, and political change, we find the rise of displaced groups that perceive their past security or dominance as threatened. At the end of World War I, with the country attempting to reintegrate a military force into a civilian work force, an unstable economic condition, global political realignment, and the rise of Bolshevism, extremist activity arose to grapple with the explosive and volatile conditions. In the 1920s, with the rise of urbanization and industrialization, the rural Protestant power structure was significantly weakened due to the extensive migration of rural populations to the cities and the shift of political power centers. In the 1930s, extremist movements were popularized by the severe economic conditions of the Depression. The 1950s gave rise to the McCarthy era, with the economic trigger being the decline of America's global corporate position. The 1960s saw the rise of the John Birch Society and saw George Wallace as an answer to the decline of white supremacy.

Extremism: All or Nothing

Lipset and Raab describe extremism as anti-pluralism or monism. With the narrowing of the ideological field to one of "historical simplism," ambivalence is seen as illegitimate. Termination of pluralistic dialogue lends itself to repression because extremist ideology can't function in an environment of open exchange and criticism (1970, 6). Polarization subverts all discussion and creates a closed system where opposing views are seen as the Armageddon forces of good and evil (Lipset and Raab 1970, 487).

Lipset and Raab describe the main elements of monism as political moralism, nativist bigotry, and conspiracy theory. Implied in political moralism is the application of any "fundamental" truth that is undebatable. John Bunzel, a critic of extremism, has used the term "anti-politics" to describe any political activity that is essentially moralistic and not open to discussion. Democratic and totalitarian systems are distinguished by "politics" and "anti-politics" respectively (1970, 12).

Nativist bigotry is portrayed as antagonism toward immigrants in its narrowest definition, but depending on historical circumstances, it can mean hatred and mistrust toward any group that has become an out-group, one that has been identified as the source of current problems and unrest (Lipset and Raab 1970, 488-489). During World War I, German immigrants were seen as pawns of the hated Kaiser. In the 1920s, immigrants, especially Catholics, were associated with discord. In addition, the Bolshevik Revolution triggered nationwide panic toward anyone who represented any form of socialism or attempted unionization. The 1930s found the Jews being blamed and used as scapegoats for contemporary perturbations. War fears in the 1940s made the Japanese and, to a lesser extent, the Germans, victims of collective nationalist hysteria. McCarthyism in the 1950s identified Communists as the source of cultural malaise. In the 1990s we find domestic militia and separatist groups blaming immigrants, minorities, and government officials for current economic difficulties and loss of white middle class social status.

Nativist movements attempt to reestablish a sense of meaning with a past that is reminiscent of a better time, one that is preferred to the present condition. In the words of Ralph Linton, "Rational nativist movements are almost without exception associated with frustrating situations and are primarily attempts to compensate for the frustrations of the society's members. The elements revived become symbols of the period when a society was free or in retrospect happy or great . . . by keeping the past in mind, such elements help to reestablish and maintain the self-respect of the group members in the face of adverse conditions" (Lipset and Raab 1970, 487).

Conspiracy theories accompany every extremist movement in America and are always found in conjunction with nativist bigotry.

Lipset and Raab state that the combination of conspiracy theories and nativist bigotry opens the way to monistic repression (1970, 490). Billy James Hargis of the Christian Crusade sums up the right-wing conspiratorial fears: "A giant gangster conspiracy threatens to take away our freedom and enslave us all. . . . a conspiracy of evil that is universal in scope and unbelievably complex in nature; it's both domestic and external. . . . left-wing liberals are under a satanic influence . . . as a matter of fact the entire left-wing movement is of the devil . . ." (Lipset and Raab 1970, 473-474). The Ku Klux Klan produced a series of papers suggesting that Catholics and the Pope were behind the death of presidents McKinley, Garfield, and Harding. Their suspicions were confirmed when no autopsy was conducted upon the death of President Harding. A Klan publication claimed that Harding had been killed by "hypnotic telepathic thought waves generated in the brains of Jesuit adepts." (Lipset and Raab 1970, 139).

Extremists Feel Alienated from the Present

Lipset and Raab have developed the term "Quondam Complex" to describe the common condition of those in right-wing movements who feel alienated or estranged from the current political and social process, either in a real or perceived sense, and who have more identity with the past than with the present (1970, 487). The dislocation can be economic, political, cultural, social, or religious or any combination of these factors. The term defines a sense of helplessness and fear toward present conditions and a sense of trepidation regarding the future. Emotional fear is the primary motivator that makes people want to reproduce some sense of the past that is known and comfortable. Human beings need a sense of belonging to and hopefulness about the future. When there is a rupture of this primary need, people will respond in a variety of ways, and participation in extremist movements is one outlet that lets people act in a collective sense toward perceived injustices.

Extremist movements can become violent and anti-democratic when there is a loss of legitimacy in the social and political institutions that were designed to protect citizens from injustices. If the political and legal systems are considered illegitimate and ineffective in correcting critical situations, then participation in the democratic processes of consensus and compromise will be abandoned in favor of alternative approaches.

The world that now moves into a new millennium is a world also seen by many as chaotic and in rather frequent turmoil. Political and financial calamities seem to abound. Whether it is the collapse of peace talks and the consequent violence in the Middle East, or the disastrous economic consequences of the Asian stock market crash for nations in the Far East, or the continued controversy over affirmative action or abortion within the United States, there are many sources of confusion and despair for those already inclined toward catastrophizing about moral, political and social developments. As we shall see, those who catastrophize and are prone to participation in passive or aggressive Christian Patriot groups are inclined to have apocalyptic visions of the world by virtue of their religious beliefs. Amid the threats and corruptions of the fallible world, these "patriots" cling to the hope of ultimate redemption through glorious battle and a righteous final reckoning. Such righteous struggle may well involve a few of them in ideological- spasmodic terrorism (see the Introduction for an explanation and a definition).

Religious Beliefs Fuel Extremist Thinking

Of the religious beliefs that might incline one to catastrophic or apocalyptic thinking, the two most prominent in American religious history, based on the writings of religious practitioners and historians, appear to be premillennialism and fundamentalism. Religious historian Norman Cohn has recounted the ancient and medieval roots of the modern millennialism that has surfaced in America since the 1970s. Cohn has demonstrated how mass disorientation and insecurity fostered the demonization of Jewish people in this and earlier centuries (Cohn 1967). Further, Cohn has suggested that a major influence on the Judeo-Christian concepts of mortal combat between ultimate good and evil and ultimate salvation in apocalyptic confrontation is the teaching of the Iranian religious master Zoroaster (1995, 105-115). As Cohn argues in *Cosmos, Chaos and the World to Come* (1995), Zoroaster broke out of the ancient, static religious view of earlier cultures. That early view saw the world as forever and unchangeably locked in a terrible combat in which heroic or warrior gods, not always reliable, kept the forces of chaos at bay. Such gods were rewarded with kingly power for their successes only to have to repeat their massive efforts at withstanding the evil ones again and again. Zoroaster altered this unchangeable world view by arguing that the combat against evil was moving steadily, if with great sacrifice and effort, to an ultimate, divine order where there would be no conflict at all (1995, 227-228). Zoroaster's message in the 1500 to 1200 B.C. age was that salvation and happiness were coming. Ultimate redemption or "rapture" becomes the message of Hebrew and then Christian sects later on, as well.

As Marsden indicates in his modern history of American fundamentalism, the belief by conservative Protestants in a coming pre millennialist clash with the world's evils has been strong and steady. Marsden contrasts the intense fundamentalism in the United States with the more passive, conservative Protestantism in Great Britain. The 1920s proved a watershed for fundamentalist extremism in America. The Scopes trial created a storm of conservative religious reaction (1980, 222). Fundamentalists saw living proof that the institutions of science, education, and the judiciary were being irreparably corrupted. Further, the philosophies of Bolshevism, Darwinism, and socialism were on the march. Conservative Christians began to see a need to become politically active in order to combat these evil trends. Prior to World War I the list of evils indicating civilization's decline included only passing reference to socialism and anarchism. By 1919, however, Soviet Bolshevism was seen as a real menace. Pre millennialists' earlier prediction of Russia's threat in the end times gave plausibility to fears of Lenin's revolution.

By 1923 or 1924, according to Marsden, fears about the "Great Bear" and the evil of the premillennial era began to appear often in fundamentalist literature (1980, 208-209). Communism, socialism, and evolutionary science were developments that surely proved the decline of western civilization and the onslaught of maddening modernity. The resounding answer of the Protestant fanatics was a movement back to Bible basics and the literal teachings of the scriptures.

The End of World War I Brings Many Changes

With the end of World War I, many Americans hoped for a return to normalcy and a renewal of the old familiar patterns of life, but by mid-1919, a number of global economic and political events had turned the hope for national calm and prosperity into a national hysteria. Robert Murray identifies seven factors that contributed to the rapid rise of this national hysteria:

1) war-born emotionalism

2) desire for normalcy

3) political instability (domestic and foreign)

4) economic instability

5) the rise of Russian Bolshevism

6) the affinity of domestic radicals with Bolshevik doctrine

7) massive social unrest in the form of riots, strikes, and bombings (1964)

Americans were unprepared for the amount and pace of post-war changes in civilian life. With the signing of the Armistice on November 11, 1918, the monumental task of converting the wartime industrial system into peacetime production presented a significant problem for which the nation was unprepared. For the nine million people who had been active in war industries and the four million enlisted men, the future loomed uncertain. Reconversion and demobilization triggered substantial inflation, which by some estimates increased the cost of living nearly 100 percent from five years earlier (Murray 1964, 7). Economic conditions deteriorated with increasing labor unrest. In 1919 alone, 3,600 strikes affected more than four million workers in virtually every industry. The demands for shorter hours, higher wages, and the right to bargain collectively perpetuated the tension between workers and the business owners who had traditionally resisted government regulation and labor union growth.

War-born emotionalism translated into declarations for 100 percent Americanism. Inherent in this gasp for patriotic fervor was a deeply rooted distrust for immigrants, whose numbers had substantially increased since the end of the war. Calls to patriotism by immigrant-hating nativists were further fueled by country's reluctance to become embroiled in the League of Nations or any other international arrangement. Returning to "isolationist" policies was no longer a viable option due to the permanently reconfigured European political landscape.

The Bolshevik ideology of unwavering destruction of the capitalist system, the abolition of private property, and the liberation of the working class proletariat ran counter to everything that the democratic system of the United States stood for and struck fear into many American citizens, especially conservatives. With domestic radicals already active and seeking reforms, the emergence of a new and challenging violent ideology exacerbated an already existing social strain. The November Revolution of 1917 saw the Czar overthrown by Alexander Kerensky's Social-Democratic Party and Kerensky's government displaced in a short time by Nikolai Lenin and Leon Trotsky's Bolshevik Party. With the signing of the Brest-Litovsk Treaty, the Allied forces not only lost an ally against the Kaiser and experienced the collapse of the eastern front against the Axis forces, but the Bolsheviks called for an end to all hostilities and advocated a universal proletariat revolution (Murray 1964, 33). Hostility toward the Bolsheviks, whom many Americans felt to be dupes of the Kaiser, magnified antagonism toward domestic radicals such as the Socialist Party and the International Workers of the World (IWW) (Murray 1964, 34). American public opinion wasn't concerned with the ideological differences within the Socialist-Communist left. Any group that was in any way opposed to capitalism or the war was considered dangerous and a threat to the American way of life.

The "Big Red Scare" succeeded in refueling nativist hatred toward foreigners, especially Jews. With Jews being synonymous with Bolshevism, the nativists had a powerful propaganda tool that manifested itself in public rumors that every Jewish immigrant was part of an invading army. A Senate committee heard from a Methodist clergyman that Bolshevism in Russia was receiving support from the Yiddish-speaking sections of New York (Higham 1977, 279).

It was in this atmosphere that the dubious document known as *The Protocols of the Elders of Zion* was introduced into the United States by Czarist army officers attempting to influence governmental policy. The *Protocols* proposed a global conspiracy for Jewish world dictatorship through manipulation of financial and political systems (Higham 1977, 280). The *Protocols* are still used today as a propaganda tool of the radical right and can be found referenced in their current ideology (Aho 1995, 91).

Rapid social change, including economic fluctuations and social dislocations due to urbanization and minority migrations continued to feed anti-Semitic fears. The pre-World War I progressive optimism was gone, replaced by a general sense of disillusionment and distrust toward economic and financial systems and participation in international affairs.

Anti-Semitic sentiments appear in Henry Ford's magazine *The Dearborn Independent* beginning in May of 1920. He launches his offensive against the International Jew out of disillusionment with internationalism and because of economic crises that directly affected his empire. To millions, Ford represented the cherished values of agrarianism and individualism, perceived to be threatened by the new international order. Ford referred to big cities as "cesspools of iniquity, soulless and artificial." His distrust of financial systems is echoed in the Detroit news with, "he is the recognized crusader against the money changers of Wall Street" (Higham 1977, 283).

The KKK Rises Again

The cultural and economic discontent of the 1920s that helped trigger nativist sentiments also provided the opportunity for the Ku Klux Klan, perhaps America's quintessential nativist organization, to experience a resurgence. Post-Civil War Reconstruction provided the original impetus for white Protestant males to organize out of frustration, loss of economic control, and fear of the growth of the African American population. The KKK was always Protestant, but didn't emphasize a clear anti-Catholic attitude until its second expansion in 1920 and 1921 (Higham 1977, 291).

In a classified report of 1958, the Federal Bureau of Investigation (FBI) departs from most historians in declaring that economic conditions were not sufficient to explain the rise of the KKK of the 1920s, as they were with the original movement in the 1860s: ". . . it flourished, not as a result of social chaos, but as a commercial, promotional scheme directed by unscrupulous promoters who capitalized on various hatreds, prejudices, intolerances, and the postwar relaxation of ethics and morals in this country to create an invisible empire based on fear, violence, and secrecy. There was money to be made in this type of social racketeering" (Department of Justice, Federal Bureau of Investigation 1958, 11).

The report goes on to state that the spirit of nativism that allowed the KKK's expressions of racial and religious prejudice was rooted in earlier nativist movements. The Know-Nothing movement of the 1850s and the American Protective Association of the 1890s had a profound influence on the hysteria that provided a foundation for the re-emergence of the KKK (DOJ, FBI 1958, 11-14).

Evidence of anti-Catholic leanings is found in *Watson's Magazine* and the *Menace*. Both publications described Catholicism as a dangerous interference with American institutions because Catholics' allegiance to a foreign source could undermine the American way of life (DOJ, FBI 1958, 16).

Father Coughlin's Popularity Rises and Falls

The rise to power of Father Charles Coughlin can be directly linked to anti-Catholic activity. The Canadian-born Coughlin was working in Detroit's Catholic diocese when Bishop Michael Gallagher sent him to Royal Oak, a poor industrial suburb, to build a new church. Royal Oak was a center of KKK activity, and Coughlin found burning crosses on the lawn of the Shrine of the Little Flower (Bennett 1995, 254). When Coughlin decided to read his sermons over the radio in 1926 in an attempt to increase his struggling congregation, he soon became a success. Within six months, he was receiving four thousand letters of support each week. By 1929, he was well established in the Detroit area, and when Columbia Broadcasting Systems (CBS) linked his sermons to a sixteen-station network, he became an instant national celebrity (Bennett, 1995, 254).

His style was comforting and mesmerizing for the millions caught in the throes of the Depression. By the mid-1930s it is estimated that ten to thirty million people listened to his weekly broadcast, *Radio League of the Little Flower*, easily the largest radio audience in the world (Bennett 1995, 254). By 1933, he had ninety-six clerks responding to the eighty thousand letters and donations received each week, totally $5 million annually.

With the Depression worsening and no end in sight, Coughlin turned his attention to economics and politics. As a virulent anti - Communist and critic of capitalism, he began to show the first signs of fascist tendencies. Lipset and Raab declare, "His was America's most distinctively fascist movement in the sense that it espoused a genuinely revolutionary program built around a strong preservationist core" (1970, 167).

In 1932, Coughlin challenged President Hoover, declared him to be "the Holy Ghost of the Rich, the Protective Angel of Wall Street," and referred to financier Andrew Mellon and his associates as "banksters" (Bennett 1995, 255). With his continued controversial themes assailing the political and financial elites, he was dropped by CBS, but created his own private network of independent stations and increased his listening audience. Millions of Americans identified with his description of current conditions and found in him a lone voice of reason in these times of crisis.

Coughlin's backing of Franklin Roosevelt helped Roosevelt to defeat Hoover in the 1932 election. Coughlin stated, "It is either Roosevelt or Ruin" and said that FDR "is the new Lincoln, leading the fight against financial slavery" (Bennett 1995, 256).

Coughlin began developing an economic platform of social justice influenced by Pope Leo XIII's encyclical, *Rerum Novarum* (1891) and by Pope Pius XI's *Quadragiesmo Anno* (1931). Both documents addressed the immorality of economic domination in the hands of the few (Bennett 1995, 256).

With his organizing of the national Union for Social Justice in 1934, Coughlin announced an ambiguous and contradictory program aimed at economic reform. The sixteen points included in his monetary solution were:

1) Liberty of conscience and education

2) A just, living, annual wage for all laborers

3) Nationalization of resources

4) Private ownership of all other property

5) The use of private property to be controlled for the public good

6) Abolition of private banking; institution of a government bank

7) The return to Congress of the right to coin and regulate money

8) Control of the cost of living and value of money by the government

9) Cost of production plus a fair profit for the farmer

10) The right of laboring men to organize in unions

11) Recall of all nonproductive bonds

12) Abolition of tax-exempt bonds

13) Broadening the tax base on the principle of ownership

14) Simplification of government and lightening of taxes on the labor class

15) In time of war, conscription of wealth as well as of men

16) Human rights to be held above property rights (Leighton 1967, 240-241).

In the midst of prolonged economic despair, models proposing economic reforms were not unique to Father Coughlin. Huey Long with his Share-Our-Wealth program was firmly rooted in the Populist tradition and proposed ending poverty by giving each family $5,000 debt-free along with a pension, a home, college education for the children, an automobile and a radio. This was to be achieved by taxing the wealthy (Bennett 1995, 251).

Dr. Francis Townsend advanced a pension plan that would give all citizens at least sixty years old $200 a month if they agreed to spend it all each month. It was believed that this would put enough capital back into the economy to refuel a stagnant system (Bennett 1995, 249-250).

Coughlin's proposals, along with those of Long and Townsend, were challenges to Roosevelt's New Deal, though Coughlin had supported Roosevelt in the 1932 election. As the Depression wore on and Roosevelt showed no interest in adopting Coughlin's banking plan, Coughlin began to oppose the president through the National Union for Social Justice. Coughlin had once chided "Roosevelt or Ruin"; he now advised "Roosevelt *and* Ruin."

Because of Coughlin's continued criticism of Roosevelt and capitalism, the Catholic hierarchy attempted to silence him, but were never successful for long. His ability to articulate the hopes and fears of common citizens made him enormously popular. The paradox of his thinking was that in his attempt to reestablish local solidarity and recreate community, he proposed that the only viable solution was a form of enhanced federal authority (Bennett 1995, 258).

As his opposition to Roosevelt became more militant, his philosophy sounded more fascist. Coughlin stated, "Capitalism is doomed and not worth trying to save. . . . there is no alternative but for the government to control credit" (Lipset and Raab 1970, 1638). The further to the right Coughlin moved, the more he echoed the writings of Lawrence Dennis, the most systematic of American fascist theorists (Ferkiss 1954, 42). Like Coughlin, Long, and Townsend, Dennis was an anti-New Dealer, but he pronounced fascism the only viable alternative to combating Communism. Interestingly, Dennis stated that he didn't propagandize for fascism, but rather was a detached observer upon the world stage. Regardless of what Dennis stated as his attraction to fascism, a federal grand jury found him enough of a risk to indict him for sedition in January, 1944. He was charged with conspiring to create a Nazi world revolution by impairing the morale of the armed forces. The trial ended in a mistrial, and except for one public speech in 1949, Dennis disappeared from the public stage (Ferkiss 1954, 48-49).

Despite Coughlin's unique ability to manipulate and motivate, his persistent attacks on Roosevelt became quite costly. Most Catholics did not abandon Roosevelt. The public faith in massive relief programs such as the Federal Emergency Relief Administration, the Civil Works Administration, the Civilian Conservation Corps, the Wagner Act for labor, and many others had begun to give hope to many Americans that there was a way out of the devastating Depression (Bennett 1995, 260).

Though he lost a large percentage of his Catholic support, Father Coughlin was still at the height of his power. In June 1936, he decided to support a third party candidate in the upcoming presidential election. Along with Dr. Francis Townsend and his Old Age Movement and Gerald L. K. Smith, who had taken over Huey Long's Share-Our-Wealth movement since Long's assassination in 1935, Coughlin endorsed William Lemke of the newly formed Union Party. Coughlin clearly expected a powerful third party showing—he boasted that he guaranteed at least nine million votes, and if Lemke didn't receive them, he would cease his radio broadcasts. When the votes were counted and the Union Party tallied fewer than 900,000 votes, Coughlin retired from radio (Lipset and Raab 1970, 170).

He ended his retirement after only six weeks and was back on the air with aggressive fascist-oriented broadcasts. He attacked labor movements as being Communist and criticized Governor Frank Murphy of Michigan for not using government troops to crush a General Motors strike. In the May 28, 1938, issue of his magazine *Social Justice,* he declared Mussolini as its Man of the Week. In July 1938, he reprinted the *Protocols of the Elders of Zion* (Lipset and Raab 1970, 171). With his praise for Nazi "social justice" programs and reprints of speeches of the Nazi propaganda minister Joseph Goebbels, he soon became a favorite of the German-American Bund meetings and was praised in the Nazi newspaper *Der Stuermer* (Bennett 1995, 263-264).

His continued drift to the right and his endorsement of the German invasion of the Soviet Union permanently eroded his popularity. His public career ended in 1942, when *Social Justice* was charged in violation of the Espionage Act and was banned from the mails (Bennett 1995, 266). To avoid putting Coughlin on trial, the attorney general asked Archbishop Mooney to silence him. Under the threat of defrockment, Coughlin retired (Lipset and Raab 1970, 171).

Nativist Organizations Proliferate

The socioeconomic and political discord occurring in the 1930s continued to provided fertile ground for a plethora of nativist organizations. Morris Schonbach estimates that one hundred to eight hundred such organizations were active during this time. An accurate number is difficult to determine because many groups were in name only, while others were inherently unstable and active for only a short time (Schonbach 1958, 8-9).

Amid the diversity of nativist activity, three groups are of particular interest because of their strength and ability to coordinate mass membership.

The Black Legion was formed by ex-Klansmen, primarily in the industrial centers of the Midwest states. The tenets of the Black Legion included supporting God, the Constitution, and an ongoing holy war against Catholics, Jews, and Negroes. As with many nativist movements, they were organized around militaristic, hierarchical, and authoritarian guidelines; their membership was estimated to be around forty thousand (Lipset and Raab 1970, 157-158). Michigan authorities conducted surveys of several hundred Black Legion members and found them to be primarily unskilled laborers with limited education, previously from the South, who were uncomfortable with urban life and afraid their employment was at risk from the rising tide of immigrants (Lipset and Raab 1970, 159). The characteristics of the Black Legion membership exemplify the demographics and describe the fears that motivate nativists during any time in our nation's history, including the present.

Reverend Gerald B. Winrod and his Defenders of the Christian Faith were a second important nativist movement. A fundamentalist preacher from Kansas and a successful circuit-riding orator, Winrod concentrated his attacks on Roosevelt as an agent of Communism and the Jews. Catholics were enemies as well, being in alliance with the Jews. He became a true believer in the Nazi cause after a trip to Germany in 1933 (Lipset and Raab 1970, 160).

Winrod demonstrates a classic paranoid personality: completely consumed by an extensive fear of the Jewish conspiracy as a predominant historical force. He believed that Jews were responsible for everything from liberalism to urban sexual decadence. Hitler was the only person capable of saving Western civilization from the Jewish scourge. One of the more interesting conspiracies that Winrod resurrected was the belief in the Illuminati as a sinister covert global force created and manipulated by the Jesuits. In his thinking, St. Ignatius Loyola, the founder of the Jesuits, was a Jew, and the Jews, Catholics, and Communists were allied to destroy fundamentalist Protestantism. The assassination of Huey Long was blamed on the Jewish-Catholic conspiracy because the assassin was a Catholic of German Jewish origin (Lipset and Raab 1970, 161).

The number of Winrod's followers was estimated at around 100,000 based on the circulation of his magazine, *The Defender.* His only attempt at politics came in 1938, at the height of his power, with a failed attempt at the Republican nomination as a senator from Kansas, in which he was able to win only 22 percent in the primary.

The third example of nativist movements is William Dudley Pelley's Legion of the Silver Shirts. Pelley's movement was a mixture of nativism, mysticism, and fascism. Pelley openly advocated fascist dictatorship, the use of violence, and the suppression of trade unions, and he used the backing of industrialists to secure his power (Lipset and Raab 1970, 162).

Pelley's early years were dominated by the influence of his father, a Methodist minister, and by his desire to become a writer. He did become an accomplished writer, with several novels, hundreds of short stories, and several movie scripts to his credit. In April 1928, while on retreat in the Sierra Madre mountains, Pelley described what he referred to as "the physical experience of dying and visiting eternity" (Portzline 1965, 8). As a result of this life-changing experience, he began publishing a magazine devoted to mystical teachings, *The New Liberator.*

His writings during this mystical period were so vague as to be almost comical. He predicted a "Dark March on Washington" by thousands of internal and international mischief-makers, and that "the economic havoc will, probably, continue to the night of September 16, 1936" (Portzline 1965, 11). Regardless of the validity of his mystical writings, his publishing activities were financially successful.

To understand Pelley's blending of fascism with "militant Christianity," we must first review the five basic tenets of fascism described by Arthur Steiner:

    1) the rejection of democracy

    2) a dictatorial technique

    3) repression of individual freedom

    4) repression of organized labor

    5) a reactionary perspective

An emphasis on dictatorship through a repressive militarism is the primary focus in Pelley's writings. His desire to combat the "alien spoilers" explains why he organized his Legion of Silver Shirts in a paramilitary style (Portzline 1965, 24). Any persons who desired enlistment had only to believe in the Constitution, militant Christianity, and the militaristic glories found in the earlier history of the United States (Portzline 1965, 26). Pelley saw no contradiction in his Christian fascist hybrid form of government, because Christ was the leader of a militant crusade, and the Silver Shirts were committed to "seeing God in every forward movement" (Portzline 1965, 27). Pelley went so far as to say that even Hitler went into the Bavarian Mountains to "get his orders from the Hierarchy of Presiding Dignitaries who meet and counsel with him." He alleged that Hitler then took these divinely inspired orders and continued "fighting the fight of international Christianity against predatory Atheism" (Portzline 1965, 31).

Pelley rejected the passivist tendencies of mainstream Christians by referring to them as "the mollycoddle Christians" whose belief in a nonviolent philosophy was "ignoring the Christ that lashed the money changers and dove sellers from the temple with the rigorous force of his literal right arm" (Portzline 1965, 27).

In 1939, with the effects of the Depression still being felt, Pelley wrote *No More Hunger,* proposing a sweeping economic plan that he termed "Christian economics." His plan included forming the United States into one gigantic corporation for whom everyone would work. Each person would be rewarded according to his or her individual contribution. In describing Christian economics, Pelley stated, "It does not make the gigantic error of assuming that all men are truly born free and equal or are entitled to equal privileges and possessions merely because each has a head, two arms and two feet." The government would grade people by occupation, and Negroes, Indians, and aliens, who, said Pelley, "are improvident and shiftless and should be made wards of the state" would be put into a caste system (Lipset and Raab 1970, 164). The chilling likeness to Hitler's Final Solution provides us with a terrifying vision of Pelley's world view.

The parallels in Pelley's, Hitler's and Benito Mussolini's political and economic expressions can be summarized in three themes:

1) the citizens in a democracy are not really sovereign

2) parliamentary governments are unwieldy and inefficient

3) governments should be ruled by an elite who can best determine and provide for the welfare of the people (Portzline 1965, 47).

The philosophical origins of support of anti-democratic themes can be traced to the writings of Niccoló Machiavelli, Robert Michels, Gaetano Mosca, and Vilfredo Pareto. Social organization is determined by the political force of a dominant or ruling class that knows what is best for the masses. Democracy is organizationally weak, with power being dispersed, and no true action can be taken because of this splintering of power (Spitz 1965, 44-45).

Pelleys' attack on democratic institutions, claiming that "the rank and file of officeholders and representatives were mainly nonentities as leaders because they were primarily motivated by a desire for money and prestige," was echoed by both Hitler and Mussolini (Portzline 1965, 52).

Despite the powerful rhetoric of Christian militancy and Christian economics in a thinly veiled fascist format, Pelley proved to be a failure as a leader; membership in his Silver Shirts never exceeded fifteen thousand (Bennett 1995, 246).

In April 1942, Pelley was arrested by the FBI and charged with publishing seditious materials under the Espionage Act of 1917. Throughout the trial, he declared his innocence and stated that his only crime was "the open castigation of Communistic Jewry and the indictment of a predatory Yiddish banking crowd" (Portzline 1965, 254). Regardless of his pleas of innocence, the jury found him guilty, and he was sentenced to fifteen years.

Into the 1950s and early 1960s, millennialism remained an important theologic belief of many Protestant fundamentalists. Concern with "rapture" or salvation, however, took a backseat to the struggle to confront and defeat worldwide Godless communism during the Cold War. Gerald L. K. Smith, Billy James Hargis, Father Coughlin, and, in a less extreme vein, Billy Graham, made opposition to the "evil empire" a top political and religious priority (see Bennett 1995).

McCarthy and the Birchers Denounce Communism

Senator Joseph McCarthy's rise and fall illustrated the cyclical nature and vicissitude of anti-communist zealotry at the highest levels of social/political institutions. Cameron Hall has well illustrated the xenophobic message and anti-democratic tactics of McCarthyism (see Hall 1954). McCarthyism contained all the elements of a religious "restoration movement" or counter-revolution, shrouded in political accusation, innuendo and terror. The movement had a message—a call for the return to sacrosanct principles of free enterprise and unilateralism. The movement had a messiah in McCarthy and several ardent disciples, including Roy Cohn, the members of the John Birch Society, and the Young Americans for Freedom.

The John Birch Society of 1999, more polished in presentation and public relations than in Senator McCarthy's time (1950s), lavishes its listeners and adherents with great conspiracy theories regarding much of American domestic and foreign policy. The Council on Foreign Relations[1] directed foreign policy for Clinton and Albright much as it did thirty years ago for the dreaded Nixon and Kissinger team. Pure constitutional government has been subverted in the U.S. Further, the twin beasts of international law and international organization (e.g., the United Nations and the International Tribunal on

War Crimes at the Hague) have worked to subjugate American constitutional government, striving to end American political sovereignty altogether. Alas, the spirits of Woodrow Wilson and Wendell Wilkie have triumphed, and the ill-fated concept of "One World" is fast approaching, according to Birch spokespeople.[2]

The reader should take note here that the notion of sovereignty is central to the beliefs and actions of Joe McCarthy and of a number of the radical groups discussed in this text. Those who have opposed federal regulation of national resources and lands do so in part because they see state and local governments, indeed individual citizens, as truly "sovereign" over property and resources. Those who, like the Birch Society, oppose the United Nations, do so in great part because they see it daily "usurping" American national sovereignty, with its so-called peacekeeping and other efforts at globalization. Those who, like the American Renaissance movement of Jared Taylor (see Chapter IV), fear and oppose greater immigration from Asia and Latin America, do so because they see traditional American culture overrun by foreigners and the political power—the sovereignty—of the traditional white majority lost both symbolically and, in years to come, literally. The militia, such as the Militia of Montana, feels that the defense of sovereign Constitutional government has slipped from the hands of the proper, unorganized citizen's militia of the eighteenth and nineteenth centuries to the professionalized, bastardized National Guard of the twentieth. A common concern among all of these groups is simply the loss of power—the loss of sovereignty. They see the country as having been subverted, led by the nose, as it were, by other powerful forces or groups.

As Jack C. Plano and Milton Greenberg (1993, 25, 556) recount, sovereignty is the idea that a nation-state is supreme within its borders, independent, and free from external control. It is this last aspect of the sovereignty concept—freedom from external control—that the reader should keep in mind when assessing the events, individuals, and groups discussed herein. The radicals of the right believe that control has been or is fast being lost to sinister, unconstitutional, un-American forces. By legal means, through vigilant preparedness, by use of arms for some, the forces gaining control and ruining sovereignty for our nation, our states, and our people must be defeated.

McCarthyism added to the zealous defense of sovereignty an apocalyptic vision by accentuating the desperation of the struggle against communism and creeping socialism. Enemies abounded, were close by, and were gaining the upper hand in American life, as the political and religious McCarthyites saw it. The movie business, the New Deal, the State Department, the United Nations, even the United States Army were feared to contain agents of the international communist conspiracy, or at least willing fellow-travelers. The "demon" of atheistic communism had to be stopped and would be stopped even if this required a final nuclear holocaust or a political coup or assassination. (Recall the some of the movies of this era: *Advise and Consent, Doctor Strangelove, Fail Safe, Seven Days in May*)

The discrediting of Senator McCarthy by the press, the president, and the public as a result of the Army-McCarthy hearings removed the messiah and dampened the tactical zeal of the McCarthy movement, but it did not eliminate the sense of desperate struggle among adherents, especially the fundamentalists, nor did it quench their thirst for a final apocalyptic confrontation with the world's evil. The Cold War rolled on, and at times, as with Berlin in 1948 and 1961, Cuba in 1962, and the Middle East in 1967 and 1973, it seemed to be rolling slowly but surely toward a dramatic, confrontational finish. By 1983, a very conservative president, one whose political skills were shaped and altered by his leadership of the Screen Actor's Guild during the McCarthy inquisitions, could cast the old foe, the Soviet Union, in now unabashed theological terminology. The "evil empire" roamed the world and America herself was vulnerable, according to Ronald Reagan.

The Fall of Communism Doesn't Stop Extremist Thinking

Impartial observers or religious novices might interject at this point that if so many of the apocalyptic fears and tensions of the years 1920 through 1990 were directed toward the religious "Beast" exemplified by the communist Soviet Union, then surely such fears and tensions were severely reduced or eliminated with the collapse of international communism and of the "Beast" itself in 1990-1991. The apocalyptic preachers and writers have hardly missed a beat, however. As contemporary messenger Pat Robertson of the *700 Club* indicates in his aptly titled *The New Millennium* (1990), the country desperately needs to promote "Bible-based constitutional government . . ." because otherwise chaos and doom are waiting just on the horizon for the countries of Europe that have newly won freedom from communism (1990, 47). America herself remains at great risk without the threat of the Soviet "Beast." God's people must, according to Robertson, redouble their efforts to establish a Christian presence in the major social and political institutions of the nation or it will be unable to recover from its spiritual and moral decline until after God's apocalyptic judgment is rendered (1990, 182).

In this millennialist faith may be seen, therefore, the scriptural prophecies of fundamentalist ministers, the ruthless and/or self-serving tactics of opportunistic politicians, the trepidations of a fearful, emotional flock of believers, and also the rantings, ravings and violence of the misguided and paranoid haters. Recently, paranoia and hate have been demonstrated tragically in terrorist acts and threats on a small and large scale. The next chapter of this book will examine some case studies of recent sporadic domestic terror problems in the United States. The events, individuals, and groups discussed and assessed in that chapter represent an illustrative, though small, sample of the extremist movement in its various configurations in the country today. Analyzing the sample will allow a fair understanding of the nature, complexity, and reach of the extremist movement.

What Attracts People to Extremism?

Before turning to events, people and groups, let us say something about how individuals come into contact with or are attracted to extremist causes in the first place. Already, we have described the patterns of hate for others, confrontational tactics, and apocalyptic and often ethnically bigoted religious views manifested by extremists throughout American history. What, however, comprises the "fatal attraction" of individuals to the extremist lifestyle? What is the nature, if you will, of their "original sin"?

Perhaps no researcher has devoted more time and effort to a firsthand pursuit of the answers to these questions than Professor James Aho of Idaho State University. In the course of writing two exceptional books on right-wing Idaho radical groups (*The Politics of Righteousness,* 1990 and *This Thing of Darkness,* 1994), Aho had countless interviews with members of Christian Patriot and other radical-right groups and corresponded by mail with many others, including some already incarcerated for misdeeds. The attraction to extremist groups seems to be partly esoteric fascination and partly a way to establish or solidify relationships with influential others. Getting caught up in the rituals, attire, symbols, and performance of extremist groups is an emotional release for many, it seems. Having relatives and/or friends who are a part of the radical group is also an important factor. For males, having a father, grandfather, uncle or brother in the organization becomes critical to their own thinking and acceptance (Aho, personal interview, 28 April 1999, Idaho State University, Pocatello, ID).

In his seven years of studying the American anti-government movement, investigative journalist Joel Dyer has brought further clarification to the issue. In Dyer's assessment, rural economic calamities in recent decades, together with literalist and prophetic religious doctrines, have influenced many otherwise law-abiding citizens to gradually accept the notion that something drastic must be done, by force of arms if necessary, to change or remove the corrupt government responsible for economic failures and the decline of moral, Constitutional values. Fundamentalism or Christian Identity teachings about God, the Bible, the Constitution, and the country have provided the religious justification for the rural disaffected and alienated—those in economic constraints already—to unite and rebel against the sinful federal government (Dyer 1997).

The authors conclude, then, that not unlike participation in political parties and other so-called mainstream political organizations, the attraction to join extremist groups is one part desire to join what seems to be a high and important drama and one part politics and socialization of friends and neighbors. The politics and socialization processes are, however, radicalized by the combination of economic frustration and religious fervor that recruits to political extremism have experienced in their lives. The feeling of participation in something of special importance and of acceptance into an already known identity with relative political comfort are both involved in the individual's decision to participate in an extremist group.

It is strange but true that in contemporary times, even groups or lifestyles that appear in many ways wholesome and good may develop a radical or violent fringe. For example, nineteen-year-old Andrew Moench, a committed Straight Edger, has been charged with participating in the killing of a fifteen-year-old youth who did not respect his philosophy. Straight Edge advocates espouse totally clean living, abstinence, and vegetarianism. Some, like Moench of Salt Lake City, are violently intolerant of those who practice contrary beliefs. In Utah alone, some forty cases of arson, vandalism, and assault are being investigated in relation to Straight Edge adherents. The Straight Edgers, identifiable in part by bold X's marked on their hands, have also become active in Canada (Susan McClelland, "Straight, but with an Edge," *Macleans,* 17 March 1999, 33).

Sadly, the attraction to extremist groups all too often becomes "fatal"—destructive and ruinous to the individual's life and to the lives of others in the community. The following chapter deals with some destructive, confrontational, and hateful acts of political extremism and includes profiles of individuals and groups caught up in the "high drama" of radicalism in the United States.

Notes

1. The Council on Foreign Relations is an intellectual group that publishes the journal *Foreign Affairs* in New York City, New York. This centrist-to-liberal publication includes the views of a variety of foreign policy scholars and practitioners. The board of advisers of *Foreign Affairs* boasts former public officials such as Ted Sorenson and scholars and analysts such as Fouad Ajami and John Lewis Gaddis, among others.

2. Observations and conclusions concerning the Birch Society are based on scanning the Society's web site at http://www.jbs.org/ and also heavily upon observation by author Rodgers at a Birch Society meeting that included a speech by Birch staffer and journalist William Norman Grigg at the Holiday Inn, Pocatello, Idaho, May 10, 1999.

Chapter Discussion Questions

1. Describe how beliefs in millennialism by religions groups have affected their view of the world and of political trends in America and abroad.

2. Describe and discuss the general impact of British Israelism (Christian Identity faith) in American Protestant thought and practice and on "extremist" political and social attitudes.

3. Discuss his sentiments against democratic capitalism and the rise to prominence of Father Coughlin; what events or ideas were significant in his rise and fall?

Suggestions for Further Reading

Aho, James a. 1994. *This Thing of Darkness*. Seattle: University of Washington Press.

Cohn, Norman. 1970. *The Pursuit of the Millennium,* Revised and Expanded Edition. New York: Oxford University Press.

Cohn, Norman. 1995. *Cosmos, Chaos and the World to Come*. New Haven, CT: Yale University Press.

Dobson, Christopher and Ronald Payne. 1982. *The Terrorists,* revised edition. New York: Facts on File, Inc.

Fuller, Robert. 1996. *Naming the Antichrist*. New York: Oxford University Press.

Hoffer, Eric. 1951. *The True Believer.* New York: Harper and Row.

Hofstadter, Richard. 1965. *The Paranoid Style in American Politics.* (First paperback edition). New York: Knopf.

Marsden, George M. 1980. *Fundamentalism and American Culture.* New York: Oxford University Press.

Robertson, Pat. 1990. *The New Millennium.* Dallas: Word Publications.

CHAPTER III

Recent Terrorist Events

"The anatomy of patriotism is complex. But surely intolerance and public irresponsibility cannot be cloaked in the shining armor of rectitude and righteousness."
—Adlai E. Stevenson. 1952. "The Nature of Patriotism" (campaign speech before the American Legion national convention, New York City, 27 August).

Having analyzed the sociopolitical environment of hate and fear in America in the 1990s, we now turn to a more pointed investigation of recent, dramatic terrorist actions in the U.S. and an assessment of where these events figure in the milieu described above. We will illustrate that these recent events fit within the category of ideological–spasmodic terrorism and spring from a climate of social and political fear and hatred and the general decline in political efficacy. Organized extremist groups—militia, neo-Nazis, white supremists, Klansmen, Freemen and survivalists—reflect a number of the problems of large, complex systems headed toward overall dysfunction. Furthermore, acts such as the bombing of the Murrah Building in Oklahoma City illustrate the manifestation of social/political system problems in the extreme. Before we turn to an examination of recent domestic terrorist-type actions, we will summarize the sociopolitical climate within which these violent and/or threatening acts exist in contemporary America.

Those problems which seem to fit with current times and the anti-government groups:

1) Inability of individuals to understand or comprehend the nature of change in the nation and the world.

2) Persistent feelings of racism and racial distrust in many parts of the country.

3) Resurgent American nationalism that is often exhibited in defensive or hostile ways toward those who are non-Anglo and/or non-Christian.

4) Decline in public approval and public faith in the institutions of government and in traditional American political processes, (i.e., decline in political efficacy—general belief that involvement in the political process will make a beneficial difference to the citizenry).

5) Increasingly bureaucratic solutions and bureaucratic rule-making as the sociopolitical system tries to respond to change, problems, and threats.

6) Persistent tendency for splits and division within American Protestantism, producing often more extreme, rigid, and uncompromising groups.

7) Increasing ability of anti-government groups to recruit, to communicate, and to coordinate their public responses to events via the Internet.

8) Increasing difficulty for the sociopolitical system to predict, prevent, or effectively respond to attacks and violence directed against major institutions.

The inability of many in modern American society to understand or deal constructively with social change is reflected, in the political sense, by the organized groups which have emerged since the 1970s devoted to fearful reaction to international, national and regional events which seem to have spun beyond their control.

As an example, consider the evolution in the politics of hatred[1] and resentment by Lyndon LaRouche and his followers. Born into a prominent Quaker family in 1922, LaRouche originally gravitated to the politics of the radical left. A Marxist for nearly two decades, LaRouche later became a leader in the Students for a Democratic Society (SDS) in opposition to the Vietnam War (Coates 1987, 200).

In 1973 LaRouche reached a turning point, as his politics moved from that of resentment and radicalism to conspiracy theories and the political theater of the bizarre. Becoming convinced that the Soviet KGB had put out a "hit" on him, LaRouche began to see international conspiracies everywhere. Jewish bankers ran the drug trade with the supervision of the British royal family. Communists controlled a succession of presidents starting with Carter. Nuclear war was seen as imminent and the only salvation was to speedily colonize Mars. All of these warped theories were put forward by LaRouche and his followers (Coates, 201).

LaRouche in the 1980s caused a major stir in California and in Illinois. During the 1986 elections in California, LaRoucheans were able to get 700,000 voters to sign a referendum petition on the state ballot that would have formally stigmatized those with the AIDS virus. Those affected would be declared "infectious" and reported to the police—a Hitler-like tactic for isolating and scapegoating AIDS patients (Coates, 203).

Also in 1986, Illinois Democratic primary voters were lulled into voting for LaRouche candidates for secretary of state and lieutenant governor, forcing the head of the ticket Adlai Stevenson III to abandon the Democratic ticket to run officially as a third party candidate for governor instead. The LaRouche "capture" of the Democratic nominations resulted in the defeat of the unwitting Stevenson and the two LaRoucheans (Coates, 204).

While LaRouche's organization suffered massive blows due to federal court orders seizing the group's assets in order to pay for outstanding fines in the nature of $16 million (Coates, 202) and due to LaRouche's subsequent prosecution and imprisonment, the anti-Semitic, conspiratorial politics of LaRouche is echoed today in the extremist work of Willis Carto and the Liberty Lobby. Carto, long a defender of LaRouche, reaches out to the believers in conspiracies through the publication the *Spotlight* and, according to the Southern Poverty Law Center's (SPLC) *Intelligence Report,* Summer 1998, with the radio work of Tom Valentine, host of "Radio Free America" for Liberty Lobby.

Perhaps equal in concern to the attention given once to LaRouche and now more so to Liberty Lobby, is the belief held by substantial numbers of farmers in the Midwest that sinister Jewish and Trilateral Commission[2] forces were responsible for farm problems. A major 1986 poll conducted by Lou Harris for the Anti-Defamation League found that 75% polled in Iowa and Nebraska agreed that both Reagan and the "big international bankers" were responsible for the farmers' troubles. Further, the Trilateral Commission and "Jewish bankers" were found to have culpability in the farm crisis for many. Twenty-seven percent expressed the thought that "farmers have always been exploited by international Jewish bankers . . ." Moreover, 45% of those over sixty-five accepted that Jewish bankers were behind their troubles! Forty-four percent of those polled who never finished high school accepted this anti-Semitic view as to the collapse of family farms (Coates, 195).

The substantial resentment over and fear about who's controlling major economic and political events is today continually tapped into and perhaps reinforced by the barrage of conspiracies and hate politics disseminated by talk radio programs like that of Tom Valentine and the Liberty Lobby as mentioned above. For example, through the *Officer Jack McLamb Show,* Mr. McLamb, a retired Phoenix, AZ, police officer, warns of a coming civil war[3] in the U.S. and seeks the help of law enforcement officials, military people and participants in the Patriot movement on his shortwave broadcast. Also, the well known William Pierce of the neo-Nazi National Alliance pushes his ideology of racial distrust, anti-Semitism, anti-gay and anti-government politics via radio broadcasts on *American Dissident Voices.* These and other broadcasters are monitored and chronicled by the Southern Poverty Law Center in that organization's *Intelligence Report.* According to an SPLC article, broadcasts by Patriot and hate groups have been put out on 366 AM and 40 FM and shortwave stations. Air time and extremism in the quality of broadcasts has increased and flourished since modest beginnings in 1990 (Carla Brooks Johnston, "Radical Radio Redux," *Intelligence Report* Summer 1998, 17-18).

Fear and resentment in contemporary American politics are a definite option it sadly seems for those who see their lives and livelihoods under the control of others and moving/changing in ways that cannot be comprehended easily or accepted. Fear and resentment are present in the works of radical political gurus such as LaRouche and in the radio barrage of Liberty Lobby, officer

McLamb, and the ever present Pierce. The politics of hate, if you will, runs often in the ideological stream of racism and racial intolerance.

Racism Brings About Incidents

There are unfortunately many incidents in contemporary American life which illustrate the persistence of racism in this country. Later in this chapter, for instance, the reader will see the summary of the ruthless, racially motivated murders committed by neo-Nazi Jim Burmeister, a soldier stationed at Fort Bragg, NC. More recently the nation has witnessed a racial crime described by President Clinton as "shocking and outrageous"—the brutal killing of African American James Byrd, Jr. near the town of Jasper, TX. Three whites, Lawrence Brewer, Shawn Berry, and William King, were arrested and charged with dragging Byrd to his death behind a pickup truck on a country road in Texas early in the second week of June 1998. The perpetrators have all served time in prison and bear connections to the racist prison gang, the Aryan Brotherhood ("Race killing in Texas fuels fear, anger," *USA Today —Nation, Internet,* 11 June 1998, 1). In July 1998, the three suspects were indicted on capital murder charges for Byrd's slaying ("3 whites charged with murder in black man's dragging death," *Minneapolis Star Tribune,* 7 July 1998). In February 1999, King was convicted of capital murder in the incident and sentenced to die by lethal injection; of the two other suspects, Brewer and Berry, Brewer was convicted and also sentenced to death by a Texas jury, while Berry received a life imprisonment sentence for his conviction.

As the Byrd killing sadly illustrates, the race hate and race crimes which so plagued the country during the Civil Rights era (1950-1970), during the 1920s, and during the Reconstruction Era after the Civil War, resurfaced in the 1990s. Recently, a South Carolina jury awarded $37.8 million in damages to the Macedonia Baptist Church, a black church in rural Clarendon County, SC. The Baptist church, which was torched in June 1995 along with a black AME church in the region, was burnt in an apparent effort by the Ku Klux Klan to initiate a "race war" by Klan members. The jury award exceeds that made against the neo-Nazi White Aryan Resistance (WAR) in October 1990 for its involvement in killing an Ethiopian student in Oregon ("Klan ordered to pay torched black church," *Reuters, Internet,* 25 July 1998). Needless to say, racism remains a significant motivator for the crimes and violence we see continually assaulting the lives and rights of many members of the minority community in our country. Racism provides fuel and drive to sustain the anger, bitterness and resentment for those in the majority community who somehow feel alienated, aloof, dislocated, or threatened by the circumstances and trends of contemporary society.

In terms of sheer numbers, 1999 (the last year for which numbers were available) saw some 7,876 U.S. hate crimes reported, including 17 murders, with 4,295 of these crimes considered to be racially motivated and another 829 based on ethnicity or national origin (*Times of India—Online* [www.timesofindia.com], 17 February 2001 account of most recent FBI statistics). Comparatively, hate crimes reported have trended down since 1997. These statistics also compare with nearly 9,000 hate crime incidents in 1996 and 7,947 reported in 1995 (U.S. Department of Justice, FBI, CJ INFO Services [online], "Hate Crimes Statistics," 19 May 2000 and Rebecca Leung, "Hate Crimes in America," *ABC NEWS.com,* 17 June 1998). According to the FBI "Hate Crime Statistics," for 1997 race-bias crimes constituted 4,710 of the 8,049 hate crimes reported. The FBI breakdown for hate crime incidents indicates that 70% of the hate crimes reported were committed against people. Intimidation was the most common type of hate crime at 39% of all such offenses; while property damage, destruction and vandalism constituted 26% of hate-based offenses and simple and aggravated assaults were at 18% and 13%, respectively (CJ INFO Services [online] "Hate Crime Statistics," 19 May 2000). Race/hate crimes are unfortunately persistent and significant in this country.

If the evidence of the numbers and the cases above were not cause enough for concern, consider also that it is believed that the numbers actually reported to the FBI merely scratch the surface of the real problem with race/hate in America. A comparative study of hate crimes done by the Canadian Justice Department concluded, after examining hate crimes in Canada, the United Kingdom, and the United States, that approximately only 1 out of 10 hate crimes are ever reported to the police by citizens in the first place. Further, police are sometimes reluctant to classify crimes involving people of different races as race/hate crimes if other material factors (e.g., money, contract disputes, familial difficulties, etc.) seem to intervene (see *Disproportionate Harm-Hate Crime in Canada,*

Internet, 15 August 1998). Race/hate crimes are somewhat like an ugly, not-too-distant, cousin whose behavior we would prefer to ignore if we could or avoid altogether by choice. Like the cousin, race/hate is present; it has shown signs of growing and becoming more serious by the late 1990s; it shatters our tidy realities; it shows no sign of going away.

Loss of Faith in Political Institutions Spawns Unrest

The American public's loss of faith in political institutions and processes has been well established. As political scientists Frantzich and Schier have documented, from the Watergate era of the early 1970s to current times, much less than a majority of the public could be said to have a substantial amount of confidence in Congress (the people's body) as an institution. Indeed Congress, though with respect to elections is most representative of the American people, is evaluated lower by the citizens than the presidency or the unelected Supreme Court (1995). Moreover, presidents have also suffered in the often harsh glare of media coverage, investigations by independent counsels, and the climate of expectations and events that move beyond even their control. As presidential scholar Louis Koenig has illustrated through an examination of Gallup Poll results on presidential approval/disapproval, presidents today tend to begin their term in office with a much shallower reservoir of good will than was true of say, Truman, Eisenhower, or Kennedy (1996, 96-97). Their base of die-hard supporters is narrower and the predictable erosion of support they experience as they near the end of four or eight years in office is a troublesome and often significant problem for them. They cannot rally the partisans behind them successfully; they have not the clout to make effective "deals" as needed with Congress or important compromises with domestic and foreign interests. Bloodied in the political fray, they often limp home wounded; this happened to Truman, Johnson, Nixon, Ford, Carter, and Bush (Kennedy's assassination; relatively favorable approval for Ike and Reagan as they finished their second terms and Clinton's steady high approval rating—59% as of Gallup's April 28-30, 2000 poll—provide the exceptions to the general trend of popular displeasure with presidents; *Gallup Organization—Princeton, Internet* 19 May 2000).

Despite the relatively happy times in terms of public mood and economic conditions, and the public's approval of President Clinton which prevailed throughout his two terms, the support for political institutions remains shaky—the current level of satisfaction for some aspects of political life may be a house built upon shifting sand. Consider for one that the disapproval of Congress, the legislative wing of government, is usually high. By May 1998, Gallup ran up the approval rating for Congress by the public at an anemic 44% with 48% disapproving of the institution. Indeed, it is fascinating to note that in relatively good times or bad Congress, as an institution, rarely catches a break with the public. Recent Gallup surveys about the Congress indicate that in 1993 and 1994 Congressional approval ratings were mixed in the 20% range, pulling up into the 30% range in the period 1995-1997 in the so-called Gingrich era (the sole exception was January 1997 when Congressional approval reached 41%). Since 1998 Congress has managed ratings in the 40% or 50% range, dipping to a low of 37% though in September 1999 and achieving a high of 57% in February of 1998 ("Congress Job Approval." *The Gallup Organization— Princeton, Internet [www.gallup.com/poll/trends/ptjobapp-Cong.asp]* 19 May 2000). Even pollsters for Democratic and Republican presidential candidates in the 2000 campaign found the public's mood anxious and apprehensive, somewhat difficult to read and assess ("Polling shows U.S. optimism fades," *Idaho State Journal,* 11 May 1999, A4).

The American public is often critical and skeptical of the institutions of government. Perhaps this wariness of the government is also reflected in the voter apathy and disillusionment that exists in this country. Of all the major industrial democracies, the United States, at between 50-55% turnout in presidential years (35-40% in off-year congressional races), has the lowest voter turnout of any. Great Britain can manage 70-80%, typically, while countries like Sweden, Norway and Australia are consistently at 80% and above (see O'Connor and Sabato 1995, 534-535 and Jackman 1987, 420). Thus, Americans are often ambivalent about politics and prone not to see the institutions and processes of politics in a very favorable light over the long term. Citizen displeasure with government is often directed toward the federal government due to its very size and bureaucratic nature.

The nature and function of the federal bureaucracy is a particular source of great irritation and a flashpoint for opposition among right-wing extremists and militia-types in the United States. The so-called "patriots" in the rightist movement see bureaucrats as agents of what has become an unelected, uncontrollable, and unconstitutional monster, trampling on the liberties of good citizens. Moreover, today "patriots" are apt to see these U.S. bureaucrats as the accomplices in a vast international conspiracy centered in the UN and in world financial institutions. This conspiracy is determined to create a "New World Order" of domination over true Americans and reflects the coming of the Antichrist, who must be resisted in an all-out manner by the purposeful "patriots."

Said "patriots" comprise a loosely connected coalition of a variety of different groups in the United States. Tax protestors; home schoolers; fundamentalist Christians; Constitutionalists represent the moderate faction of the patriots opposed to much of the present-day authority and intrusion of the federal government. The hateful, extremist side of the "patriots," however, is comprised of neo-Nazis, white supremacists and assorted militia survivalists, who tend to be well-armed and ready at a moment's notice to defend against or respond to the perceived sinister encroachments of the government in Washington and coming evils of international government (Jill Smolowe, "Enemies of the State," *Time* 145 (19), 8 May 1995, 62).

Growing Bureaucracy Engenders Displeasure

While bureaucracy is a source of sinister work according to the "patriots," it has been developed often out of seeming necessity and, certainly, public and political choice over our country's history. As political scientist James Q. Wilson has so eloquently written, political choice has been critical to the decisions to increase, decrease and reform bureaucratic agencies over the years (1986, 132-147). Virtually no "bureaucratic state" existed in America at all in our first 150 years as a republic. Agencies began to be established in significant numbers as a result of the tripartite calamities: World War I, the Great Depression and World War II (Wilson, 125-126). To be sure, the rise of bureaucracies, as Wilson has studied them, parallels the growth and subsequent demands of specialized interest groups in the U.S. However, choices and demands by citizens (e.g., veterans after the Civil War; farmers during the Depression; civil aviators in the War years; oppressed groups like Native Americans) have resulted in the creation and expansion of bureaucratic power on the whole (1986, 125-149).

The roots of the current intense hatred of federal bureaucracy could perhaps be traced all the way back to George Mason and the Anti-federalists at the time the Constitution was ratified if we had unlimited time and wished to be mostly philosophical about the subject. For our purposes, however, we may see the foment against the feds as erupting with significance in two protest movements of the 1970s: (1) the Antiproperty Tax Movement in California and (2) the "Sagebrush Rebellion" prevalent in Nevada and surrounding mountain and western states.

Analysts David O. Sears and Jack Citrin have described the tax revolt movement of the 1970s in California as evidence of a "populist insurgency" (1986, 261). Led by Howard Jarvis, disgruntled Californians successfully created and passed the Proposition 13 ballot initiative, designed to limit the growth in property taxes and assessments each year. Prop 13 was a direct response to the frustrations of commercial and individual property owners to the substantial increases in property taxes experienced during the '70s because of highly inflated real estate values. Inflation, in general, was a significant problem and in the double digits, nationally. Sears and Citrin (1986) argue that the rebellion against the tax system in California was significant beyond the politics of that state. The effort spawned similar tax initiatives in at least 6 other states. Three of these—Massachusetts, Idaho and Texas—succeeded in passing their tax limitation ballots (262).

Further, the movement against taxes may be seen to fit within the broader context of American politics. Prop 13 set the stage for the rugged-individualism and economic competition stressed by Ronald Reagan as president (Sears and Citrin 1986, 279). Nationwide and even in Congress, politicians and citizens alike emphasized the need to curtail growth in government at every level. The military, as it turned out in the Reagan approach, was initially exempted from this emphasis on slow growth or status quo budgets. By the Clinton-Bush contest of 1992 both candidates and both major parties (and a significant third party if Ross Perot's Reform group may be included for that year) embraced the philosophy of a balanced budget and leaner, more effective and efficient government. By 1998, Clinton and the now Republican-led Congress would find that their chief "policy" dispute seemed to be over how to distribute the surplus in federal money which had accrued over a decade of slow growth/no growth budgeting. Indeed, the political landscape had changed and a big part of the push for change, a part which stimulated and reinforced the notion that government is out of control and must be tamed, was Proposition 13 in California.

A second significant movement in the 1970s which unleashed the "hounds" of resentment against federal agencies was the so-called "Sagebrush Rebellion." The movement erupted in Nevada and neighboring Idaho in 1978 and 1979 as a loose coalition of miners, ranchers, timber interests, and small-town businesses came to the front in opposition to the efforts of Idaho U.S. Senator Frank Church and environmental groups like the Sierra Club to try to preserve and protect major wilderness areas in Idaho and the West from development. In Nevada the state legislature even went so far as to claim lands owned and managed by the federal government. In particular, the Western opponents of federal control were livid over the operation and methods of the federal Bureau of Land Management. Small-town residents whose livelihoods seemingly depended on the irrigation, grazing, recreation and tourism associated with the use of federal lands were violently opposed to further wilderness protection or use restrictions. Sagebrush coalition advocates were particularly unwilling to compromise on their two main goals—stop further federal restriction on the land and ultimately return control over the vast acreage of federal land in the West to state and local governments (see Ashby and Gramer 1994, 590). Indeed, as early as 1968 Senator Church was receiving letters from constituents praising Nevada's stance on the federal lands issue and bemoaning the "double sovereignty" federal ownership and management was said to have brought within the state of Idaho (see Frank Church papers. Series 7.5. Box 1. Folder 3. Special Collections, Albertsons Library—Boise State University).

Sagebrush participants may have lost out in the accomplishment of their goals in the short run (the Carter administration succeeded along with Church and others in significantly expanding federal wilderness acres through congressional legislation, such as the River of No Return Wilderness law of 1980 for the Salmon River country of Idaho). These "rebels" succeeded, however, in bringing to the front the underlying state and local resentment toward the feds in the mountain region, and they kept it there. They caused long-time Senator Church great grief, for instance, in his reelection fight against Steve Symms in 1980. Church ultimately lost, in a close election. His seniority in the Senate and his work on natural resource issues were not enough to offset the dual efforts of the National Conservative Political Action Committee (NCPAC) of Arlington, VA, and the Idaho-based "Anyone But Church" Committee out of Boise at a time of Sagebrush opposition to federal encroachment and when the conservative presidential candidate, Ronald Reagan, was making much headway against Jimmy Carter because of America's supposed decline in national defense and increased vulnerability (see Frank Church papers. Series 5.6. Box 2. Folder 6. Special Collections, Albertsons Library—Boise State University, for documents and correspondence targeting the Senator and his responses to such targeting).

Some of the philosophical kinsmen of the Sagebrush warriors and the inheritors of their no-compromise stance versus the federal government are the militia members, "Freemen," and disaffected of the 1990s (see for example the profile of Samuel Sherwood in Chapter IV). Indeed, the county rule movement, which asserts local control over even federal and/or state lands within the county, mirrors the Sagebrush Rebellion in motivation and resentment of higher authorities if not in political tactics (see Junas 1995 for a description of the convergence of the county rule and militia movements highlighting the example of Catron County, New Mexico). One Utah resident rather neatly summarized the philosophy of the former Sagebrush rebels and the current anti-government crowd in 1978 as espousing opposition to communists, to dishonesty in government, and to agencies of the federal government, such as the IRS, the Bureau of Land Management (BLM), and the FAA, among other things (see Frank Church papers. Series 7.5. Box 2. Folder 3. Special Collections, Albertsons Library—Boise State University). Thus, a certain individualist, independent, often bitter, opposition to the government in Washington permeates the radicalism of the right in the American West. To be against Washington, to say "no" to its goals and operations, has been and still is something of a political badge of honor.

That badge of honor has helped to define the approach of political leaders of the West, such as former Congresswoman (or "Congressman," if you will, since her campaign web site indicated that is her preferred referent) Helen Chenoweth (now Chenoweth Hage since remarriage). Known for her opposition to federal natural resources regulations and her advocacy of landowners' and business owners' property rights, Chenoweth has, by her speeches and her service, become increasingly admired by the right-wing radicals of the West. A former aide to then Congressman Steve Symms, Chenoweth is featured as she delivers a long, detailed speech critical of environmental regulations (equating with Marxisim some current ones like wetlands protection) in a video recently produced and released by the Militia of Montana. Citizens must not, according to Chenoweth's view, be kept from, ". . . our beloved earth." Use of resources and not protection of same is the goal of Chenoweth and of others, including radicals from the mountain states (see *Chenoweth for Congress,* web site *http://www.helen chenoweth.org/* for Chenoweth's preferred title and Chenoweth, "America in Crisis," *Militia of Montana* (videotape), Noxon, MT, housed at General Curriculum Collections, Albertsons Library— Boise State University. Boise, ID, 1998).

In the wake of the Oklahoma City bombing in 1995, the federal Justice Department estimated that at least 35 counties, primarily in Arizona, New Mexico, Nevada and California, had declared their authority over federal lands within their borders. A National Federal Lands Conference in Utah was organized to foster resistance to federal regulation and control over federal lands. In Nevada the resistance has at times been aggressive and even violent. On the Fourth of July 1994 a Nye County Commissioner named Dick Carver took to a bulldozer to forcibly open a road the U.S. Forest Service had closed. In 1995 bombs destroyed on one occasion a personal van and on another the office of former Forest Service Supervisor Guy Pence in Carson City, NV (Erik Larson, "Unrest in the West," *Time* 146 (17), 23 October 1995, 52-54). Hence, the flames of opposition sparked by the Sagebrush Rebellion of the 1970s remain hot and searing in many parts of the West today. Militia and other so-called "patriots" have garnered sympathy and at times tacit support for their anti-federal stance from the disaffected land owners and ranchers of the intermountain region (Idaho, Montana, Nevada, Utah and Wyoming).

Religion and Political Extremism

The relationship between religion and political extremism in modern America may be seen in developments within fundamentalist Protestantism. In so far as the divisions within Protestantism and the tendancy toward splits and the creation of more rigid and extreme groups, a few major points should be made. First of all, divisions within the Protestant camp abound. In his seminal *Encyclopedia of American Religions* (1978) J. Gordon Melton provides a brief synopsis of some 498 Protestant affiliations, churches or groups in the United States. Generally, these religious bodies fall, according to Melton's assessment, under one of 10 families of religion, exclusive of Mormons. These families are: Lutheran, Reformed-Presbyterian, Liberal, Pietist-Methodist, Holiness, Pentecostal, European Free-Church, Baptist, Independent Fundamentalist, and Adventist. For Melton these families are comprised of the primary Protestant believers in the country, having no liturgical or priestly traditions such as those found among Roman Catholic, Orthodox, and Anglican/Episcopal parishioners (Melton 1978, Introduction and Table of Contents). Baptists, the single largest general grouping of Protestants in America in terms of overall numbers, have at least 55 separate sects, according to Melton's survey.

It is no wonder that division exists in a sense; the basis for Protestantism is the notion of individual pursuit of faith and the formation of a personal relationship with God, without the aid or direction of earthly intermediaries such as priests or the binding quality of church rules. Acceptance of the Bible (often followed literally) as the guide to a good life and of Jesus Christ as the personal savior of all believers are the fundamental teachings of Protestant groups. Thus, there are almost more splits and re-splits in Protestant churches, looked at historically, than one can keep track of. For the purposes of our work, two general groups of fundamentalist Protestants in America have significance for the so-called "patriot" movement: premillennialists and the Christian Identity (British Israelite) group. Each of these groups has been described in a historical context in Chapter II of this book; the impact of the theological beliefs of premillennialism and British Israelism has been largely accounted for. Both of these groups have contributed much to the fear of the present and future and the hate toward "others" not unlike the white majority which we see acting out extremism in America in many of the ways described in this text (see also profiles of Robert Millar, Richard Butler, and Pete Peters in Chapter IV for the impact of religion on extremist views and actions by "patriot" leaders).

Hate Groups on the Web

The Southern Poverty Law Center (SPLC) reports annually as to the number of "hate" groups that are active in the United States in each state and also the number that maintain web sites for purposes of communication and contact. According to a recent Internet edition of SPLC's *Intelligence Project* (17 May 2001), 1999 saw the existence of 602 active, race/ethnicity based groups advocating hate. Many violent acts were either planned or carried out by these groups. Race/hate groups included some 110 Klan Klaverns, 180 Neo-Nazi groups, 39 activist Skinhead groups, 32 Christian Identity (racialist religious bodies), 48 Black separatists, 88 Neo-Confederate groups, and 105 other groups, which include a patchwork of philosophical, media or militia advocates who spread race/hate (May 2001). The number of active "Patriot" groups was found to be 194 in 2000, according to the SPLC's web site, also. "Patriot" groups included 72 militias, a few "common-law courts," and numerous other associations, correspondents and publishers. SPLC insiders define "Patriots" as those who are opposed to the "New World Order" or advocate or adhere to extreme antigovernment ideas. They may not, however, follow violent or racist practices (*Intelligence Project,* 17 May 2001).

These perpetrators of race hatred and political extremism are able to espouse their beliefs, coordinate efforts, and recruit new adherents through the use of at least 163 web sites on the Internet. In their efforts today they frequently target children and adolescents with strong visuals, music, cartoons, and catchy phrases (SPLC, "163 and Counting . . . Hate Groups Find Home on the Net," *Intelligence Report* Winter 1998).

One of the web sites which illustrates the problem and prominence of the use of Internet resources by extremist groups is the White Nationalist Links. As logged on by one of the authors in August 1998, White Nationalist Links contained a listing of some 70 white nationalist, extremist, and other supportive groups (e.g., White Aryan Resistance (WAR); Church of Jesus Christ Christian, Aryan Nations [2 sites]; ALPHA.org; Scriptures for America; Nation of Europa; etc.) The text of the page indicated that all sites had been updated and tested as of February 11, 1998. The bottom of the text contained a caption statement which continually flashed to the reader—"White Revolution Is The Only Solution!" Beneath that caption read the words, "We must secure the existence of our People and a future for White Children" (*White Nationalist Links, Internet* [updated 11 February 1998] 14 August 1998).

Accessing two of the many sites listed on the *White Nationalist*

Links, produced the following sampling of information. ALPHA.org actually represents a web network of white nationalist groups itself. The newest addition to ALPHA.org's list of groups to access was *Aryan Graphics,* symbolized by a swastika. Some groups on ALPHA.org such as Aryan Nations also appear on *White Nationalist Links.* Others, such as *Posse Comitatus,* do not. ALPHA.org even includes a site termed *Aryan Dating Page,* where white, "gentiles only" women can be identified for dating white, "gentiles only" men and one may even log onto a prison pen pal through the dating page (SPLC, *Intelligence Report, Internet* Winter 1998). E-mail is of course possible to ALPHA.org. One site within ALPHA.org which was accessed for more extensive information was CNG (Cyber Nationalist Group) (ALPHA.org. Links to other organizations, 14 August 1998).

CNG's "Suppressed Facts Page" (II) indicates that CNG is "An Anti-Homosexual, White Nationalist Organization" wanting, so the statement goes, to encourage independent thinking and telling those who disagree to "go crying to the *nanny state* for help" (14 August 1998). CNG offers many opportunities for readers to access information and interact with other like-minded "patriots." Essays, art, comic strips, computer games, and a newly devised discussion forum are available, for instance.

Back to the White Nationalist Links and one finds some interesting and troubling information through the link *White Pride World Wide* (WPWW.com). *WPWW* (14 August 1998) indicates that its purpose is "to highlight what's beneficial to the white race, and what's detrimental to the white race." One thing definitely detrimental (our research has shown this to be a real "bogeyman" for "patriot" groups, along with the "New World Order" and Zionism) is multiculturalism. *WPWW* wants all readers, regardless of sex or age, to know the detriment to the future of the White race which is being done in the name of multiculturalism.

Throughout the initial pages of *WPWW*'s web site one finds a listing of radio broadcasts with topical summaries by Dr. William Pierce, head of the white nationalist National Alliance and author of the now infamous *Turner Diaries* under the pen name Andrew MacDonald. These broadcasts are devoted primarily to white-nationalist or related issues (e.g., whites are losing the majority in America; what would have happened if Germany had won the war; Jewish gangs [alleged by Pierce] to be forcing women into white slavery in Eastern Europe; etc.) (WPWW.com, 14 August 1998, 5-14). Focus upon recounting lists of the so-called conspiracies and harms committed by Jews is prevalent on the *WPWW* web site; included is a list of Clinton administration officials who are, according to *WPWW*'s jaded and distorted views, "The Jews that Run America" (14 August 1998, 13).

That these web sites exist at all and that (as the authors can attest) they are so technically polished and visually well-done is certainly cause enough for concern as to the state of ideological thought via the Internet in this country. That these sites represent only a small sampling of what's available to the reader is downright scary! As one can gather by what we've presented, extremism is alive and flourishing and, today, extremist thinkers and actors have a very sizable network of technological and informational resources to access in order to fuel and to fan the "fires" of hate and distrust. As recounted in his significant assessment of extremist-group computer usage, Matthew Zook has summarized the five major ways in which computer networks enhance the capacity of militia movements as follows: 1) computer networks act as alternative news sources for militia folk; 2) slickly produced web sites create a sense of equal legitimacy for all information presented, from the absurd to the reasonable; 3) networks provide unaffiliated information users with greater access to militia propaganda; 4) networks reduce isolation for scattered, unorganized militia sympathizers and adherents; and 5) computer access offers a means of communicating objectives, strategy and tactics within the decentralized militia movement (1996).

The synopsis of the Oklahoma City bombing of April 1995 which follows later in this chapter is evidence of the sociopolitical system's difficulty in predicting, preventing or responding to terrorist attacks within the climate of serious distrust of the federal government and of racial and ethnic minorities in America. Unfortunately, the bombings of American embassies in East Africa on August 7, 1998 have also driven home the condition of vulnerability of government interests abroad in a most tragic way. Car bombs partially destroyed or damaged American embassies in Kenya and Tanzania, destroying surrounding structures and killing a total of nearly 250 people, including 12 Americans, and wounding over 5,000 (John O'Callaghan, "Tanzanian suspects freed as bomb probes continue," *Reuters, Internet,* 15 August 1998). The initial group to claim responsibility for the acts to date was the otherwise unheard of "Islamic Army for the Liberation of Holy Places," which indicated in messages sent to radio and television stations that they wanted the release of certain Islamic clerics, including Sheikh Omar Abdel Rahman, a blind Egyptian religious leader serving a life sentence in the U.S. for his involvement in the initial plot to destroy the World Trade Center in 1993 and other public facilities in New York ("Islamic group claims anti-U.S. attacks, vows more," *Reuters, Internet,* 8 August 1998). The federal investigation into what took place and who's responsible continues; evidence points, apparently, to a terrorist ring managed and financed by the rebellious Saudi millionaire Osama Bin Laden. Fearing further attacks on Americans and convinced that the evidence found during arrests, interviews, and police raids pointed unquestionably to Bin Laden, President Clinton ordered cruise missile attacks on Bin Laden's area of operations—training and support facilities in Afghanistan—and on a chemical producing facility in Khartoum, Sudan (Lawrence McQuillan, "U.S. says attacks aimed at stopping new bombings," *Reuters, Internet,* 20 August 1998). It remains to be seen as to what the outcome of this probable protracted conflict against Bin Laden's group will be.

In the wake of the embassy bombings, terrorism expert after expert has called attention to the vulnerability of American assets to single-minded groups devoted to destruction. These commentators, such as the well-known Brian Jenkins, echo the ideas put forward in an emphatic way by terrorist specialist, Peter Probst at a 1997 Department of Defense anti-terrorism conference in San Antonio, TX. Probst was critical of American anti-terrorism efforts for their inability to predict changes in the tactics and operations pursued by terrorists. Biological and chemical attacks have not been well anticipated or planned for, according to Probst. More effort, Probst believes, should be made to conduct effective "wargame" tests of the security measures in place at military facilities. Also, Probst argues that an anti-terrorist institute, to include psychologists, cultural anthropologists, language experts, historians, and cross-cultural communications experts, needs to be established in order to better build a knowledge base about terrorists and potential terrorists (Douglas J. Gillert, "Terrorism Expert Sounds Battle Cry," *Armed Forces Press Service, Internet,* 1 April 1998). As Joseph Douglass, Jr. and Neil Livingstone put it back at a time when the Cold War was still on—a question that remains central to effective anti-terrorism today—"How do we understand who is doing what to whom, and what defenses or alternative responses can best help preserve the desired order (1987, 178)?" American policymakers are still today struggling to respond to this fundamental question, over a decade later.

Having sketched out the basic problems exhibited by today's sociopolitical climate, we now turn our attention to several mini-case histories of right-wing terrorist and terrorist-like actions from America in recent years. Riley and Hoffman outline five potential types of terrorist organizations in the U.S. in their study of state and local terrorism preparedness. They are: 1) ethnic separatist and émigré groups; 2) left-wing radical groups; 3) right-wing racist, anti-authority, survivalist groups; 4) foreign terrorist organizations; 5) issue oriented groups (1995, 13). Of these five, the authors have chosen to concentrate upon the recently active and volatile right-wing, racist, anti-government and survivalist types in the remainder of this work, including the following case studies. The first case examined is the Oklahoma City bombing.

Oklahoma City Bombing

Melissa Erhard and Mickie Bennett were having a cigarette and sharing an interest in Melissa's new dog outside the Journal Record Publishing Company in Oklahoma City, OK, when, on April 19, 1995, they noticed a yellow Ryder truck parked across the street and in front of the Alfred P. Murrah Federal Building. This was at about 9:00 in the morning. At 9:02, as it has been said of volcano eruptions, sudden spring blizzards, and tornados, "All hell broke loose." The routine of the nearby workers had been utterly shattered by a "roaring" blast and a shower of dirt and rocks. Erhard was later treated and released from Midwest City Regional Hospital for a burst eardrum and cuts and bruises. She was a survivor; 168 occupants of the neighboring Murrah Building were not so fortunate (Bryan Painter, "Co-workers experienced Blast Close-up," *Daily Oklahoman,* 19 May 1995, 1-2).

The impact of the Murrah bombing was literally the jolt felt "'round the country," if not the world. One hundred sixty-eight lives lost, suddenly and without warning, many of them children in the building's day-care facility. Personal and public loss due to the blast was overwhelming. According to early estimates, financial costs totaled $652 million in losses to the governments and the private sector, including approximately $34 million in loss to the state of Oklahoma. The damage assessment as of May 1995 placed federal losses at $225 million; Federal Emergency Management Agency (FEMA) costs at $33 million; potential private insurance reimbursement at $105 million; and the remainder in unfunded costs to the tune of $289 million (Paul English, "State Struggles to Find Money for Bomb Costs," *Daily Oklahoman,* 19 May 1995, 1). The ongoing trial and appeals process of the two arrested, tried and convicted in relation to the bombing, Timothy McVeigh and Terry Nichols, will be lengthy and costly, not to mention emotionally taxing to the victims and family and friends of the victims of the fatal blast.

Aside from the financial and time and energy costs associated with the bombing and court proceedings, significant costs may be seen in the sacrifice and suffering of those who somehow survived the destruction of April 19, 1995. Brandon Denny's case illustrates the kind of impact we refer to. Brandon, 3 years old at the time, and his sister Rebecca were among the children at the day-care center on the second floor of the federal building. Brandon was taken to Presbyterian Hospital with massive injuries and doctors doubted his chances of survival. A hole the size of a quarter was bored into Brandon's skull by fallen debris. A protrusion of brain tissue had to be removed which resulted in hampered speech and limited mobility on his right side. Gradually, Brandon recovered facility of limb and attention. Jim Denny, Brandon's father, expressed the feelings of people related to those who did survive: feelings of anxiety, frustration and even the guilt that comes with being one of the few to survive. Parents of children killed in the devastation, such as Edye Smith, whose two sons perished, assured the Dennys that they had nothing to feel guilty about (Carla Hinton, "Boy's Recovery Reflected in His Grin," *Daily Oklahoman,* 2 June 1995, 1). Such was the emotional havoc wreaked by the terrorism of 1995.

The costs, financial, human and psychological, resulting from the April 1995 incident tell part of the tale of the impact of the event, a very sad and tragic part. The other part of the story which needs to be told is the account of how the bombing resulted in changes in governmental responses and changes in public policy toward terrorism.

On Wednesday, June 7, 1995, the U.S. Senate passed the Anti-terrorism Bill by an overwhelming vote, 91 - 8, initiating a process which would culminate in final approval of this significant legislation and important changes in government policy toward domestic terrorism. The bill (S. 735) ultimately passed the Congress on April 18, 1996, in a compromise form which disappointed many of its original backers, including Rep. Henry Hyde (R-IL) the House sponsor of the legislation. A loose coalition led by the ACLU, conservative Republican House members, and the National Rifle Association (NRA) objected to numerous features of the Senate bill which they claimed provided for overly intrusive law enforcement tactics in the areas of wiretaps, use and release of evidence, and increased law enforcement powers in relation to suspected terrorists (John E. Yang, "House Votes to Remove Controversial Provisions From Anti-Terrorism Bill," *Washington Post* [Internet—*Legi-Slate* Article], 14 March 1996). Senator Bob Dole, chief sponsor in the Senate, successfully beat back attempts to restore controversial amendments to the final bill in order to secure final passage of the Anti-terrorism and Effective Death Penalty Act of 1996. (Greg McCulloch, *Legi-Slate* News Service bulletin, 17 April 1996).

Oklahoma Governor Frank Keating, himself present at the ceremony wherein President Clinton signed the anti-terrorism act into law, gave great credit to the relatives of victims of the Oklahoma City bombing for their repeated trips to Washington, D.C. to lobby for tough anti-terrorism bills (Hon. Frank Keating, *Speaking Frankly Homepage,* week of April 29th1996).

President Clinton supported the anti-terrorism law, strongly at times, and said in his signing ceremony on April 24, 1996 (just over one year past the day of the OKC bombing) that a "mighty blow" had been struck against those who would perpetrate political violence (John F. Harris, *Washington Post* [Internet—*Legi-Slate* Article], 25 April 1996). Clinton, always in favor of a comprehensive legislative approach to the terrorist problem at home and abroad, even came to embrace features of the April 24th law, such as restrictions on appeals by death-row inmates, that he was skeptical about in the climate of American concern and sentiment toward the victims and survivors of the Oklahoma bombing and their affected families.

As to the story leading up to the Oklahoma City bombing, this is illustrated by the saga of Timothy McVeigh and his apparent accomplice, Terry Nichols. According to CBS News (*Terror on*

Trial, 25 March 1997) McVeigh had a youthful and long-lasting fascination with weapons and with survivalist techniques. In his high school days he was maniacal about being a soldier. Joining the army, he served the country and government he would later come to hate in the Persian Gulf War. Ambitious in his chosen profession, McVeigh had the desire to become a Green Beret. Testing for this field, McVeigh was judged by the army to be unfit for it. It seems that the combined effects of lost weight and fatigue, together with the stress from his Gulf War service, made the soldier unable to qualify for the Special Forces (Jones and Israel 1998, 49). It was rumored that McVeigh failed the psychiatric portion of the Special Forces tests, but this issue has been hotly disputed by McVeigh's attorney, Stephen Jones (1998). McVeigh had proven adept at sol-diering during his service in Desert Storm, winning an Army Commendation Medal for his battlefield work. He was unhappy and unable to accept his inability to become a Green Beret. He did, however, voluntarily sign a statement of withdrawal from the Special Forces program (Stickney 1995, 116-118).

After his army experience, he began down the steady path of anti-government, militia-style extremism. Along this path McVeigh encountered the Nichols brothers and militia influences of Michigan and of McVeigh's home state, New York. He was associated briefly with the Arizona Patriots, a militia movement begun by Jack Maxwell Oliphant (Baradat 1997, 283) and wherein he encountered Michael Fortier and his wife. Fortier would later prove to be the critical witness as to McVeigh's intentions and actions resulting in the Oklahoma City bombing. Journalist Bill Wallace of the *San Francisco Chronicle* reported on April 24, 1995, some 5 days after the Oklahoma City bombing, that the Arizona Patriots whom Fortier and McVeigh were associated with had long had a pattern of vio-lence and conflict with legal authorities. Indeed, a federal investi-gation in 1986 brought about the indictment and conviction of 8 members of the Patriots for crimes including firearms infractions and planning to rob an armored car in Nevada in order to raise money for militia actions, one of which was the planned bombing of the Internal Revenue Service Center in Ogden, UT (Bill Wallace, "Arizona Extremists' Possible Link to Suspect Explored," *San Francisco Chronicle* [Internet archive] 24 April 1995).

McVeigh also developed sympathies for and ideological kin-ship with the Arkansas extremist group Covenant Sword and Arm of the Lord (CSA), created in 1976. CSA's ringleader Richard Wayne Snell was to be executed for the murder of an Arkansas state trooper on April 19, 1995, at 9:15 P.M., the very day of the Oklahoma bombing (*CBS Evening News,* 24 March 1997).

Kerry Noble, an ex-CSA member who reformed, told CBS News that CSA leadership had indicated that right-wing militias were looking for an "unlikely" target. And further, they argued that there was, "no such thing as innocent people" in the war for the soul of the American nation.

McVeigh, by all accounts, was sympathetic to the plight of the Weaver family at Ruby Ridge and very much concerned and then enraged by the government's treatment of the Branch Davidians in Waco, TX, in April 1993. McVeigh held vigil outside the Davidian Compound during the standoff and was livid over the final, deadly government assault on the religious sect. That assault took place exactly two years to the day before the Oklahoma City bombing.

Of all of McVeigh's associations, no doubt the most troublesome and significant in the world of extremism was his relationship to the Nichols brothers, James and Terry, of Michigan. It was with the Nicholses that he stayed for several different stints after his discharge from the armed service. James Nichols and his brother were among a small group of extremists who espoused attitudes of violence toward government institutions and who "renounced" their citizenship to the corrupt, "New World Order-dominated" national government. James Nichols once promised that he and an anti-government group "would be involved in the killing of cops, judges and lawyers," according to FBI testimony of May 22, 1995 ("Bomb Suspect's brother Released," *Daily Oklahoman,* 23 May 1995, 1). Agent Patrick Wease testified at a hearing that James Nichols had told a neighbor that a group called The Patriots "would take over the government by force" as soon as they had enough members. At James Nichols' hearing authorities introduced as evidence a letter from McVeigh to James Nichols indicating his plans to go to Arizona, while Terry Nichols headed to Kansas.

Aside from the personal affiliations and loyalties outlined above, McVeigh held ideological beliefs shaped by right-wing literature, especially the novel *The Turner Diaries,* by neo-Nazi William Pierce. As David Bennett articulates in *Party of Fear*, the novel describes the murder of prominent Jews and the financing of a racist revolution through counterfeit operations and armored car robberies (1995, 348). The racist paramilitary group, the Order, organized in the Pacific Northwest, indeed had attempted to carry out the gameplan of *The Turner Diaries* in piecemeal but ruthlessly effective fashion in the mid-1980s. Killing Alan Berg, Denver's talk radio personality, robbing armored cars in Seattle, WA, and Ukiah, CA, and counterfeiting in 1983 and 1984, the Order, also known as the Silent Brotherhood, followed Pierce's scenario closely until the FBI made the Order a top priority in 1984. Leader Robert Jay Matthews died in a federal shoot-out, while accomplices Bruce Carroll Pierce (who killed Berg) and Gary Yarborough were stymied by arrest, trial and conviction (Bennett, 1995, 349). In perhaps a brutal irony, McVeigh was stopped by an Oklahoma state trooper on Interstate 35-North outside Oklahoma City after the bombing and a copy of a passage from Pierce's novel was found in his car.

While the government's case in the Oklahoma City bombing centered on McVeigh and his friend and alleged accomplice, Terry Nichols, the possibility remains (as was strongly argued by McVeigh's legal defense team) that others were also involved, perhaps in a prominent way. Federal authorities recognized the possibility of a conspiracy which went beyond the two arrested. In the grand jury indictment of August 10, 1995, the phrase "others unknown" is used in relation to the charge that McVeigh and Nichols conspired and plotted with "others unknown" to carry out the devasting crime in Oklahoma City (Jones and Israel 1998, 99).

The bombing of the Murrah Building for which McVeigh was convicted and sentenced to die by a federal jury in Denver, CO, in June of 1997 seems to have been the sad culmination of the ex-soldier's turn toward racist, anti-government ideology and the politics of violence and aggression in America. Terry Nichols was convicted on a lesser charge of conspiracy in relation to the planning of the Oklahoma bombing and later sentenced by Judge Richard Matsch to life without parole one year after McVeigh's death sentence was pronounced (Jones and Israel 1998, 311). In February 1999 a 3-judge panel of 10th Circuit Court of Appeals upheld Nichols' punishment; similarly on March 8, 1999, the U.S. Supreme Court refused to hear the appeal of McVeigh, who had lost his appeal to the Circuit level in the fall of 1998. Nichols' plight was further sealed when the full panel of the 10th Circuit Court rejected his claims for appeal by April of 1999. (See Howard

Pankratz, "Nichols' Appeal Rejected" and Laurie Asseo, "McVeigh's request for appeal dies," *Denver Post Online,* 27 February and 9 March, 1999 (accessed 28 May, 1999 and also, [Denver] *Reuters News Service,* "Full Panel Rejects Appeal In Oklahoma Case," 1 April 1999). A state trial process for capital murder proceeds for Terry Nichols in Oklahoma. Nichols' appeal of the states right to try him separately from the feds remains at the discretion of the U.S. Supreme Court. Timothy McVeigh once asked for a new trial based on the assertion that his original defense attorney, Stephen Jones, improperly leaked information to the press regarding McVeigh and failed to properly represent McVeigh's interests (see *Minneappolis Star Tribune,* 8 March, 2000). McVeigh later halted all further appeals on his behalf and was scheduled to be executed in a federal facility in Indiana on May 16, 2001.

The execution was delayed for 30 days upon the order of U.S. Attorney General John Aschcroft because the FBI revealed that it had not turned over thousands of documents to McVeigh's original defense team which had originally been deemed by the agency to be without relevance to the case. Bureau personnel mistakenly failed to inform defense counsel or the court of such and Ascroft's decision allowed McVeigh's new legal team (directed by Nigh and Chambers) to review the documents and file relevant motions. The trial judge in Denver denied a motion by Nigh and Chambers for a full evidentiary hearing on the materials that would give them the possibility of showing a fraud had been perpetrated on the original court by the holding back of said "evidence." Judge Matsch's decision was upheld on appeal by the 10th Circuit Court on June 7, 2001 and McVeigh waived any further appeal. On Monday, June 11, 2001, Timothy McVeigh was executed by lethal injection at the federal facility in Terre Haute, IN, at approximately 7:14 A.M. CDT. The Oklahoma City bombing, the most devastating terrorist act in the nation's history, was, however, one among many troubling, difficult and violent actions perpetrated against lawful authorities and civilians in the United States since the early 1980s.

Other Domestic Events

There are many events that could be analyzed in the course of deliberating upon recent domestic terrorism, but for purposes of time and with logic in the analysis preserved we will briefly assess four cases which seem to be similar to the Oklahoma bombing in terms of the apparent intensity of hate exhibited in the acts by the terrorist perpetrators. The four are: 1) the unresolved Atlanta bombings from the July 1996 Olympic Games through February 1997; and a similar bombing in Birmingham, AL, on January 29, 1998; 2) the murder of two black citizens as part of a neo-Nazi ritual by James Burmeister, a soldier on active duty at Fort Bragg, NC; 3) the harassment of City Judge Martha Bethel of Ravalli County, Montana; and 4) the exploits of the "Four Corners Survivalists" during the summer of 1998. Fortunately, the Atlanta and Birmingham bombings threatened the lives of many more than were killed. They were perpetrated in an apparent effort to do great harm in the name of an ideological cause and to the direct detriment of ideological enemies. So, too, was the bombing in Oklahoma. The North Carolina murders were done by a white, middle-class average male who after high school became enmeshed in neo-Nazi beliefs, lore and ritual. Burmeister sought out the military as an apparent safe haven, in his case, for his extremist views. The difficulties administered to the unfortunate judge in Montana were delivered by anti-tax, anti-government militia members who, like McVeigh, have declared war on the federal government and *all* government officials who are seen to do the feds' bidding. The survivalists who allegedly killed Colorado police officer Dale Claxton and wounded three other law enforcement officials in the desert southwest were seen to be preparing for some kind of major milita-style operation versus the governmental system in the region, prior to the time that a great manhunt bore down to apprehend them for the murder and shootings of area policemen.

Atlanta and Birmingham

The Atlanta situation began with the shattering bomb at Centennial Park at the Summer Olympics on the evening of July 27, 1996. One person was killed and 100 injured in the blast.

Following the unsolved bombing at the Olympic Compound in July of 1996, Atlanta experienced two other serious, and apparently terroristic, bombings. First, on January 16, 1997, an Atlanta Family Planning Clinic was bombed injuring 7, according to numerous national news reports. An ideologically motivated right-wing group, the Army of God, claimed responsibility for the bombing via Atlanta media. Initially, there was no confirmation of the group's involvement in the bombing by law enforcement officials.

A month later, the night festivities at the "Otherside," a lesbian bar in Atlanta, were savagely interrupted by another, similar bomb. Fortunately, only one person was seriously injured by the blast. The Army of God again seemed to be connected. One over-whelming commonality for all three bombings is that each bomb used nails as shrapnel. Further, a backpack left at the scene seemed to be the method of delivery for the bombs. Plus, the Army of God claimed its own involvement in each bombing, save for the one at the Olympic Games. Recently, these identifiable patterns have led authorities to suspect that the Army of God was connected to the Olympic bombing as well as the other two.

Atlanta's Mayor Campbell asserted after the third bombing, on February 21, 1997, "We are dealing with a deranged killer." Perhaps, if indeed an extremist group is involved, Atlantans are confronting a *set* of deranged killers." (*WDN,* 23 February 1997)— deranged killers who do not hear voices or suffer from clinical psy-choses, but who are derailed and directed by a distorted, hateful and contentious ideology. An ideology of violence toward one's per-ceived enemies and intolerance of those who are different and un-American and un-Christian. With ideologies such as those espoused and practiced by the Army of God, the Order, and neo-Nazis, the Timothy McVeighs of America can, indeed, kill. January 30, 1998, witnessed the bombing of a Birmingham, AL, abortion clinic which resulted in the death of a security officer, an off-duty policeman. CNN reported on Monday, February 2, 1998, that the so-called Army of God had also claimed responsibility for this bombing.

ATF and FBI agents mounted a significant search for a North Carolina resident, Eric Rudolph, whose pickup truck was spotted leaving the scene shortly after the explosion. Tracking Rudolph led authorities to the mountains around Murphy, NC, where they found Rudolph's pickup abandoned more than a week after the January 29,1998, bombing in Alabama. It is there, in North Carolina, that the trail of Eric Rudolph went completely cold until July 1998, when Rudolph contacted a North Carolina health food store owner, took food supplies and a pickup truck from the owner, and left behind 5 $100 bills to pay the owner for the provisions. Rudolph then fled into the vast woods near Andrews, NC, causing another massive manhunt. (John Bacon, "Trail 'cold' for Clinic Bomb Suspect," *USA Today,* 15 April 1998, 3A and *Headline News,* 15 July 1998).

Fort Bragg

The Army of God and/or Eric Rudolph are perhaps illustrative of the concerted actions of extremists engaged in spasmodic terrorist activity; the actions of enlisted men Burmeister, Meadows and Wright of Fort Bragg illustrate the concerted action and beliefs of individuals zealously committed to race-hate ideas and practices. Burmeister was found guilty of the murders of Michael James (male) and Jackie Virdon (female), both African Americans in North Carolina. Seemingly, though astonishingly, James and Virdon were killed arbitrarily and willfully in order that Burmeister complete one of the supposed rites of passage into neo-Nazism: killing an African American. Jim Burmeister of Thompson, PA, seems to have led a fairly normal, middle-class life until his post-high school days. After school he was increasingly attracted to skinhead and neo-Nazi propaganda. He threatened to kill his hometown sheriff because of the sheriff's enforcement of traffic regulations. He was suspected of trying to build a bomb while stationed at Fort Bragg. The FBI notified base officers of this suspicion. Testimony at trial revealed that he did, indeed, build a bomb to use later in a racial holy war. He was found guilty of the murders of James and Virdon and sentenced to life imprisonment without parole (*48 Hours,* CBS News, 17 July 1997). Burmeister's trek into Nazism and aggression points out the destruction which even one or a few committed partisans can do. Sadly and similarly, the July 4th holiday weekend of 1999 saw a Benjamin Nathaniel Smith go on a shooting rampage against minorities in several cities in Indiana and Illinois, including Chicago. Smith, a member of the racist group the Church of the Creator based in Peoria, IL, killed an African American ex-basketball coach at Northwestern University and wounded 6 Orthodox Jews in a shooting binge in the Chicago area. In Bloomington, IN, Smith fatally shot a Korean-American male and wounded several other minorities in Indiana and Illinois before killing himself as police in Illinois attempted to apprehend him after a car chase (*Milwaukee Journal Sentinel,* [*Associated Press/Washington Post* sources], 5 July 1999, 1A and 9A) These cases also point out the vulnerability of all American institutions to bigotry and terror, even those known for codes of honor and strict discipline, such as the U.S. Army. No institution or organization is safe from terror, today.

It is unfortunate that members and veterans of the U.S. military seem to have been intensely affected by and, at times, entangled with anti-government, hate-based extremists, such as militia. Stephen Bowman relates in "Interview With a Terrorist" for his contemporary book on terrorism that some of the ex-Phoenix Group of Vietnam Veterans who periodically gather for reunions have become involved in the extremist Aryan Nations and in the Ku Klux Klan. As Bowman's interviewee stated, the former members of the CIA-based Special Forces of the Vietnam War in large numbers would have enjoyed implementing a plan to take over the U.S. government. Experience indicated to these fighting men that the country was not being run by true democratic principles, so they could rationalize that they would actually be "saving" the country. Other ex-Special Forces members supported these stark impressions. Apparently, federal agents also see ex-Special Forces members as prime recruiting targets for extremist groups (Bowman 1994, 70-73).

Montana

In our third highlighted terrorist event, the case of woes visited upon Judge Martha Bethel of Montana represents in many ways the worst nightmares of government officials confronted by the aggressive tactics of extremist militia or "patriot" groups (80-81). Presiding over a traffic violation of a Montana "freeman," the judge was presented with a 28-page ultimatum from the Montana chapter of the active North American Volunteer Militia. The judge drew attention to this militia pressure in her public statements, and matters worsened. She was threatened that her home would be shot up; that she would be hanged; she received hate mail from throughout the country; was forced to place her children in other homes a week at a time due to militia threats (Stern 1997, 80). The judge herself has advocated a no-nonsense no-compromise posture versus the militias out of the belief that to concede to these "terrorists" is to encourage and embolden them.

Colorado

The fourth event in our coverage of ideological-spasmodic terroristic situations perpetrated by or according to the requirements of an organized extremist group is the apparent shoot and run violence of the "Four Corners Survivalists." Their tactics have generated a massive, yet unresolved, search in the desert southwest where the borders of Arizona, Colorado, New Mexico and Utah meet. Survivalists Alan Pilon, Jason McVean, and the late Robert Mason are alleged to have killed Cortez, CO, police officer Dale Claxton on May 30, 1998, as he stopped them under suspicion that they had stolen a county water truck. Following Claxton's murder, two sheriff's deputies in Montezuma County, CO, and one in San Juan County, UT, were wounded in apparent confrontations with the heavily armed militia-style outlaws *Excite News,* ("Big force searches U.S. West for fugitives," *Reuters Internet,* 6 June 1998, 1-2).

On June 4, 1998 police uncovered the body of Robert Mason, who apparently killed himself with a gun, during the early days of the search for the survivalist fugitives near Bluff, UT. Mason's brother Gary indicated in interviews with authorities that Robert had distinct anti-government and anti-police viewpoints, and had gathered about him a large cache of survival equipment and weapons, even AK-47 assault rifles. Sheriff Jerry Martin of Dolores County, CO, one of those heading up the search of the summer of 1998, believed that the survivalists were initially operating according to some "master plan," which if identified would hasten the day of their arrest ("Manhunt returns to Colorado," *Reuters, Internet-Yahoo News,* 4 July 1998, 1-2). Still, the trail of the remaining survivalists, Pilon and McVean, has grown very cold (reminiscent of that of suspected Alabama bomber Eric Rudolph) and televised news reports on CNN and common thinking speculate that the two have been able to go "underground" and evade authorities due to help received from other militia-style operatives in the Four Corners region. Certainly the flat-out disappearance of Pilon and McVean in the southwest and of Eric Rudolph in the Carolinas suggests strongly that whatever has happened to each of them it likely happened as a result of the assistance of interested "others." Logic would dictate that these three best evaded arrest because they followed a thought-out plan which included help from substantial anti-government contacts in their respective regions of the country.

Less Extreme Groups and Individuals Also Exist

The foregoing examples of modern-day, militia-style actions represent the extreme tactics of a minority in the far right movement. Although a minority, the "fringe" elements commit the destructive and notorious deeds and create the public panic and consequent media frenzy which are a part of the periodic national reaction to domestic terrorism.

Yet, what the authors have learned from the research devoted to this text is that the reputed "fringe" in militia-style organizations represents merely the tip of a sociopolitical iceberg whose critical mass for the most part remains hidden from public and media consciousness. This critical mass includes those who agree with the ideological beliefs of the extremists in large part, but disagree as to tactics and the timing of their use. The mass below the public surface, so to speak, also incorporates the religious, spiritual leaders and groups who see as their mission in life the restoration of a "Christian state" in America before the final, righteous battle with the arrayed forces of evil in the world. The mass consists of countless hangers-on; "Sunshine patriots"; passive, casual protestors; constitutional defenders; and far right believers. However, significantly, this critical mass is made up of many, many otherwise ordinary, middle-class, white citizens who have concluded that their government, especially, and the modern American culture, whose values the corrupt government supports, are beyond real redemption and constitute mortal enemies to true American ideals and practices.

The white, middle-class reactionaries reflect a growing trend in expectations, thoughts, and political and lifestyle choices. The choices of this majority group, which now feels culturally and politically threatened, are described, for instance, by Jonathan Tilove in a *Newhouse News Service* article in the *Minneapolis Star Tribune* in July 1998. Citizens such as Sally Vaughn and Jared Taylor (see Chapter IV for a biographical profile of Taylor) represent a part of the critical mass of middle-class opponents of the government and of the cultural trends. Fears of liberal immigration policies, bilingual education, multiculturalism, interracial marriages, even declining birthrates among whites have had the cumulative effect of creating panic among the tense majoritarian whites in America.

Sally Vaughn and her husband, a retired truck driver, fled the cultural trends and fears around San Jose, CA, and moved to the more majoritarian Cheyenne, WY. Vaughn echoes the views of many in describing her concerns over the loss of traditional, white, middle-class culture: "Why is it wrong to want to preserve our culture and way of life?" (Jonathan Tilove, "The Coming White Minority,"

Minneapolis Star Tribune, 13 July 1998, A-5). Jared Taylor, head of a white nationalist organization called the American Renaissance, indirectly has an answer to Vaughn's question: "We [meaning the white majority] have the right to be us and only we can be us" (Tilove 1998). Taylor's Fairfax, VA, organization is dedicated to what is seen as a defense of a declining white majority. Members like Taylor fear that the whole nation is fast becoming a vast, multi-ethnic neighborhood that whites will flee from for their own smaller communities when the ethnic/racial mix significantly changes. Vaughn, Taylor and their cohorts are not aggressive or violent anti-government resisters. They do not engage in "defensive" paramilitary training to prepare for the apocalypse. They are not prone to participate in marches, protests, or active or passive civil disobedience. They fight with their ideas and sometimes with public relations efforts; they are politically aware and active; importantly, they vote with their feet, trying to avoid the cultural and political miasma that they see as poisoning the "true" America. Ironically, those such as Vaughn and Taylor are the daughters and sons of European immigrants who themselves struggled against discrimination, poverty and insensitive government agencies to eventually build stable, productive lives. That the overwhelming number of American minorities seek the same result from their own struggle is lost on Vaughn and Taylor and the others below the tip of the nation's cultural and political iceberg. Having perhaps seen America's past through rose-colored glasses, as Tilove (1998) describes it, they now "flee the future," a future they can barely stand to view at all.

Notes

1. See for example our discussion of the ideological and religious underpinnings of the politics of fear and hate in Part II of this text.

2. The Trilateral Commission was founded in 1973 by David Rockefeller, Zbigniew Brzenski and other prominent citizens from banking, business, education, government and labor. Its focus has been on debate and discussion of issues pertinent to the economic, political, and security partnership between the U.S., Western Europe, and Japan, hence trilateralism (Plano and Greenburg 1993, 563-564).

3. On July 1, 1996 federal officers arrested 13 members of the Arizona "Viper Militia" in the Phoenix area. These folks were charged with plotting for over 2 years to bomb government buildings, having held training exercises in the desert where they exploded ammonium nitrate bombs. Federal agencies and the Phoenix police were all to be targets, according to a video made by the Vipers. The work of an undercover Arizona State Police officer helped to foil this groups efforts before they could, perhaps initiate the "Civil War" McLamb and others warn of incessantly (Steve Macko, "Arizona Militia Group Arrested by Federal Authorities," Emergency Net *News* Service [Internet], 2 July 1996, 2:184).

(Questions and Suggestions for Further Reading for Chapter III appear after Chapter IV.)

CHAPTER IV

Profiles in Anger

"And generally all vain-glorious men, unless they be withal timorous, are subject to anger; as being more prone than others to interpret for contempt, the ordinary liberty of conversation: and there are few crimes that may not be produced by anger."

—Thomas Hobbes. 1651.
Leviathan (Chapter XXVII,
"of crimes, excuses, and extenuations").

Introduction

The following character sketches reflect the selective judgment of the authors as to twelve of the most influential and important leaders of the "patriot" movement, in its many varieties, over the past two decades. In some cases (as perhaps with Jared Taylor) the persons presented here may not be the most well known among the public or the mainstream American media. However, these activists and thinkers have been judged, upon analysis, to have had a substantial impact on the contemporary anti-government opposition and resistance in the United States.

Frequently, the reader will note that the term "white nationalist" is used either as a partial or whole summary description of the type of leader the individual seems to be. The authors have attempted to use the descriptions as more than mere labels or stereotypes. We have sought to inform and educate through the summary descriptions as well as the full character profile in each case. Relying upon our years of teaching in the areas of social and political thought and upon our research and analysis of the "patriot" movement in its many forms, we have concluded that nationalism and racism are critical motivators for those most active in current anti-government strategies and tactics. The term "white nationalist" is a way of bringing these two powerful drives together in summary descriptions of activists who are inclined to racial separatism and segregation in regard to religion and politics (seeing white European culture as superior) and are nationalist in their orientation toward the history, development and rightful role of the United States.

The twelve angry apostles presented in this chapter reflect many varieties in the "patriot" movement, from those who are militant and aggressive, even given to violence (see profile of Richard McLaren) to those who are more intellectual and political (see profile of Jared Taylor). A number of these individuals have changed their attitude, approach, and/or level of involvement in the anti-government movement (see profiles of James "Bo" Gritz and James J. Johnson, for example). Some individuals discussed here might well be considered very dangerous to the good public order and perhaps even socially evil. Others are rigid and intolerant or insensitive of those not like them, while still others are, as much as anything, laughable, almost comic in their acting out their off-center ideology. As M. Scott Peck has indicated, summarizing the views of Eric Fromm—who devoted his career to the study of Nazism, the creation of human evil is ". . . a developmental process: . . . we become evil slowly over time through a long series of choices" (Peck 1998, 82 and Fromm 1964; 173-178). The characters the reader is about to encounter here are, each in his/her own way, somewhere in process in the development of their particular brand of extremism and, let the reader judge, evil. Thus, these "profiles in anger" represent a sample which reflects the general breadth and diversity of the patriot movement and the evolutionary manner of life in the often radical and intense "otherworld" of the extreme right in America.

Louis Beam (White nationalist, revolutionary)

Louis Beam may be described as a hard-core activist of the contemporary radical right in America. He was indicted, along with Richard G. Butler (see Butler's profile in this chapter), David Lane, Bruce Pierce, Richard Wayne Snell, and 9 other aggressive white nationalist activists in 1987 by a federal grand jury in Fort Smith,

AR. Ten of the defendants, including Beam, were charged with "seditious conspiracy between July 1983 and March 1985," aimed at overthrowing the federal government. While charges against one defendant in the case were thrown out due to lack of evidence, Beam and 12 other defendants were acquitted on all counts by the Arkansas jury. Since sedition cases are so rare, much political controversy emerged as a result of the case. Also, the defendants' attorney, De Day LaRene, was an excellent advocate and structured the case to the advantage of his clients very successfully (George and Wilcox 1996, 344).

Racial and ethnic politics and bias undergird almost everything Beam does, says and stands for. He has been prominent writer and speaker for sympathetic white supremacist crowds and gatherings. He has used the Internet extensively; he was one of the first white supremacists/white nationalists to use the computer to establish a bulletin board network for white supremist thinkers and writers. Beam publishes a newsletter, *The Seditionist,* and has been noted for developing a "leaderless resistance strategy" for those in the white nationalist movement to follow against the forces of the "New World Order." Beam has advocated violence to respond to what he sees as the unlawful actions of the federal government and the U.N. He is reported to have created a "point" system for the assassination of federal officials and civil rights activists ("Klanwatch," *Southern Poverty Law Center, Internet,* July 1998).

In former roles, Beam acted as a leader of the Texas KKK, as a paramilitary trainer of militia-style participants, and as a roving ambassador for Richard G. Butler's Aryan Nations ("Klanwatch," *Southern Poverty Law Center, Internet,* July 1998). He argued for revolutionary action through the Internet, railing against conspirators of all stripes, but especially the CIA, Jewish groups and leaders, foreign governments, and of course, the nebulous, never-still "New World Order" movement (L. R. Beam, "The Conspiracy to Erect An Electronic Iron Curtain," *Stormfront, Internet,* 21 July 1998). Recently it was reported that Beam had fallen ill due to the effects of Agent Orange from his service in Vietnam. He is apparently out of the picture as a successor to the Aryan Nations' Richard G. Butler and it remains to be seen what active role, if any, in the extremist movement Beam will play in the future. (See *Hatewatch.* "Richard Butler," www.hatewatch.org. 3 June 1999).

David Duke (White Separatist and Nationalist)

David Duke is a former Klansman and American Nazi. Duke established his Ku Klux Klan in Louisiana in 1974. Prior to this, Duke had briefly participated in the National Socialist White People's party (Nazi). Duke is an articulate, polished speaker and he achieved substantial initial success with the Klan in Louisiana. Duke was arrested in 1976 for inciting a riot in New Orleans. He was convicted, sentenced to 6 months jailtime and a $250 fine on a first offense (George and Wilcox 1996, 370-371).

In the late '70s, Duke became embroiled in a dispute over personal, political and financial strategies for the Klan with Bill Wilkinson, a former Duke lieutenant and rival Klan leader. In 1980 Duke relinquished Klan leadership to others in the South and formed a new group, the National Association for the Advancement of White People (George and Wilcox 1996, 372).

As Connolly and Dewar of the *Washington Post, Internet edition* (18 February 1998, A05) reported, Duke ran as a Republican and was elected to the Louisiana state legislature in 1987. Since 1990 Duke has run for the United States Senate and governor in Louisiana, losing both races. Duke caused quite a stir in these two elections, taking advantage of Louisiana's unique bipartisan free-for-all primary to scare or unseat prominent incumbents. Under Louisiana's system, voters may pick from among the candidates of all qualified parties for each office in the primary vote. Then, if no candidate receives a majority of the vote for an office, the top two finishers, regardless of party affiliation, compete against one another in the general election.

Duke gave Bennett Johnston quite a test in 1990 in the Senate race before losing in November. In 1991, he bumped out the incumbent for the second spot in a crowded primary for governor. Duke was again dispatched in the general election by long-time politico and then former governor Edwin Edwards, a Democrat. Duke has a thirst for the electoral arena and the political spotlight. He ran for president on the Populist Party ticket in 1988 and attempted a bid for the Republican nomination for president in 1992. Both efforts failed to generate any real support outside Duke's own home district in Louisiana. In May of 1999 he finished third and out of the run-off in the congressional primary election to replace ex-House Speaker Bob Livingston (Curtis Wilkie, "Duke queried on mailings, invokes Fifth Amendment," *Boston Globe, Internet,* 21 May 1999).

Duke is a frequent speaker, appears on TV talk shows, and raises money for his exploits rather effectively. Recently, he was required to appear before a federal grand jury investigating the sale of his campaign mailing list to other Louisiana political candidates, most prominently Governor Mike Foster (R-LA) (Wilkie 1999).

Though Duke certainly has greater ambition than he has had political success, he is a persistent force to be reckoned with. Despite his smooth, media-wise approach, he remains wedded to white separatist, segregationist, and racialist themes. He is the "bad boy" of far right politics, who won't go away.

Rev. Robert G. Millar
(Christian Identity Spiritual Leader)

Rev. Millar is difficult to categorize because of the secluded lifestyle he, his family, and congregation lead at a remote village, Elohim City, in the wooded hills of eastern Oklahoma near the town of Muldrow. Further complicating a true sketch of Millar is the fact that so much conflicting information has been reported about him and the village by the press and by others who are former residents or knowledgeables of Elohim City. This much can be said of Millar with some certainty: He is in his 70s, married for more than 50 years, and has 8 children and numerous grandchildren. His village operates its own school (K-12) and has, internally, been without apparent violence or abuses. Millar advocates maintaining an open, positive relationship with members of the FBI and other law enforcement officials, responding to their inquiries. Millar advocates the Christian Identity doctrine of British Israelism, he says, without racism. Millar has been a great critic of the government's handling of the Davidian group in Waco, TX, of Randy Weaver and family, and treatment of the African American men subjected to untreated syphilis in the infamous Tuskegee study (Robert G. Millar, "What The Press Does Not Say About Elohim City," *Right of Israel Online,* 30 July 1998).

Among the many matters in dispute: 1) Former federal inform-ant Carol Howe, who visited at Elohim City frequently in 1994, is reported to have stated in court in July of 1997 in Tulsa that Millar was a paid informant of the FBI. Howe is not the most credible source due to the fact that her "tapes" and claims of knowledge about a conspiracy of numerous people to bomb the Murrah Building in Oklahoma City, ultimately found in court to be perpetrated by Timothy McVeigh with assistance by Terry Nichols, were never substantiated; 2) It has been reported that Elohim City is heavily armed and is a haven for militia-types, white supremacists, and radicals, but no hard, direct links exist between McVeigh or other violent-prone radicals and Millar in so far as condoning or supporting violent acts is concerned. Millar has repeatedly said the village does not shun the downtrodden or vagabond and may have provided shelter to those who went out to do harmful deeds, but that he and his flock promote and practice peaceful lives (see James Graff, Patrick E. Cole and Elaine Shannon, "The White City On A Hill," *Time,* online 149 (8), 24 February 1998 and J.D. Cash, "Bombshell. The Rev. Robert Millar Identified As FBI Informant," *McCurtain Daily Gazette,* July 1997 from www.Free Republic. Com, 30 July 1998.

Richard McLaren (Militia-style Leader; State Separatist)

Richard McLaren is the self-appointed ambassador of the so-called "Republic of Texas," hearkening back to days of independent Texas prior to statehood and in pursuit of the claims which eventually brought Texas into conflict with Mexico. McLaren alleged on March 24, 1997, that more than half of New Mexico and parts of four other states belong to the "Republic." McLaren and his group of self-styled "Republic citizens" engaged in a "paper war" against then Governor George W. Bush, state Attorney General Morales, and the State of Texas through the filing of bogus civil lawsuits and property liens ("Texas Republic Chronology," *Houston Chronicle.com* [Associated Press sources] 27 April 1997).

Leader of a kidnaping foray against innocent neighbors which began on April 27, 1997, McLaren and his more extremist faction of "Republic citizens" held hostages for days in a standoff with Texas state troopers. For his role in the kidnaping and related matters, McLaren, who ultimately surrendered, was sentenced to 99 years in the state penitentiary. Later, he was also convicted in Dallas of 26 federal fraud counts, involving himself, his wife Evelyn, and other group members. These "Republic citizens" were found guilty of writing millions of dollars in bogus checks in an attempt to purchase a Learjet, among other items. McLaren faced a life sentence and fines of up to $25 million for his direction of the fraudulent efforts of the "Republic of Texas" ("Texas separatist found guilty on 26 fraud counts," *USA Today,* 15 April 1998, 3A).

McLaren may be viewed as a militia-style state separatist who was inclined to use any available and convenient means to assist him and his group of "citizens" in accomplishing their goal of restoring the Texas Republic to its original, "independent" condition, unattached to the "corrupt" federal government.

James "Bo" Gritz (Christian Patriot-Nationalist)

Gritz is a former Green Beret, who served meritoriously in Vietnam and devoted time to unsuccessful attempts in the 1980s to trying to find supposed American POWs left behind in Southeast Asia. The highly-decorated Gritz became a leader in the "Christian Patriot" right, acting as the vice-presidential candidate of the new-styled "Populist" Party in 1988; former Klan leader David Duke was the party's presidential standard bearer. Gritz dropped out of the race once he says he "realized" what Duke's racial views were! In 1992, as widely reported, Gritz became the Populist candidate for president, gaining about 100,000 votes. During the campaign, Gritz opposed foreign aid, the Federal Reserve regulation of banking, and, the actions of the national government in general.

Gritz and one-time associate, covert operations specialist Scott Weekly, have both confirmed that in 1986 they were asked by the CIA to provide covert training operations in the Nevada desert for the Afghan Meyahedeen rebels opposing the Soviet-sponsored communist government in that country (Webb, 1998, 329).

Gritz pursued POWs thought to be left behind in Laos twice and traveled once to Burma in pursuit of information concerning POWs. In Burma, Gritz and Weekly met with opium warlord Khun Sa. Khun Sa, according to Gritz, had no information about POWs but did have knowledge about an alleged CIA-operated heroin smuggling network which had supposedly helped to finance a secret army of anti-communist fighters in Laos. Gritz claimed that Khun Sa provided Weekly and himself with names of CIA officials supposed to be involved in the heroin trade and whom the opium lord had met with personally (Webb, 1998, 339).

Gritz helped to negotiate the surrender of Randy Weaver to federal authorities at Ruby Ridge, ID, in 1992. (SeeChapter V for more on Weaver and the Ruby Ridge incident.)

Gritz operates a "Center for Action" in Nevada and publishes a "Patriot" newsletter. Gritz has distanced himself from militia groups and yet he does teach paramilitary training classes. Gritz once devoted himself to spreading his message via a radio talk show from Idaho. Through his talk show he made an appeal to fugitive Eric Rudolph to turn himself in for questioning for the January 29 bombing of a women's clinic in Birmingham, AL. Further, Gritz has indicated to CNN that he is working with the FBI to try to get Rudolph, who may have a shortwave radio at his disposal, to surrender peaceably to authorities. The FBI has not confirmed enlisting Gritz, but the right-wing leader has proven once again to be in the thick of things when it comes to anti-government incidents and possible confrontations between the federal authorities and militia-style citizens ("Bo Gritz says FBI has enlisted him in Rudolph search," *CNN, interactive* [CNN.com], 3 August 1998).

In 1994, Gritz, friend Jack McLamb, and former Arizona legislator Jerry Gillespie began the development of a "Christian Covenant Community" in a remote, mountainous area near Kamiah, ID. Those good "Christian Patriots," Gritz envisioned, who feared the approaching apocalypse and conflagration, could gather there to prepare and defend themselves. Gritz and Gillespie later disagreed over the management and parted company. The intended "Almost Heaven" retreat turned into a millstone around Gritz's overextended neck. Settlers did not always want to conform to Gritz's ways of doing things. Gritz's motivation for settling in Kamiah may well have been related to his getting more votes in Idaho in the 1992 presidential election than in any other state and also the fact of the lack of stringent building and planning and zoning codes in Idaho County, Idaho. Residents moving there seeking freedom from government regulations were then in no mood to accept much management from Gritz or his cronies. The series of eleven subdivisions in the Clearwater Valley remain somewhat segmented and uncoordinated as an idyllic community. After 1998, Gritz left the covenant residents, including his former wife, and now lives mainly at his ranch in Sandy Valley, NV, near Las Vegas. McLamb, a retired police officer from Phoenix, continues to be a presence at Kamiah, distributing his newsletter, *Aid & Abet,* which is a pitch primarily to law enforcement and military types to accept his views regarding the corruption of U.S. society, the undermining of the Constitution and various conspiratorial theories as he views them (phone interview with a coordinator/member of the Clearwater Valley Citizens for Human Rights, Kamiah, ID, 16 May 2001).

In September 1998, Gritz unsuccessfully attempted suicide, distraught over his pending divorce to his wife of many years who left him during his adventure to help locate Eric Rudolph. ("Trojan Horse, etc.," *Harvest-trust Web pages,* 1 April 1999, 1-7). One year after his attempted suicide, Gritz remarried in Oklahoma to a woman supportive of his periodic alignment with the Church of Israel, a Christian Identity Sect. In the spring of 2000 Gritz was acquitted of conspiracy and abduction charges in connection with a child custody case he became embroiled in in Connecticut when he apparently assisted a mother in freeing her sons from the custody of their father. The father was accused by his estranged spouse of sexual abuse of the boys. Repeatedly, the enigmatic Gritz has a way getting involved in assorted events of chaos, panic and disorder. In April 2000 Gritz was making public appearances again. An ad for the Oklahoma City Hall of Fame Gun and Knife Show at the Oklahoma Fairgrounds included a picture of the veteran and indicated Gritz would appear in person so that attendees could ". . . meet the most decorated Green Beret Commander" (*Daily Oklahoman,* 28 April 2000, 5-D). Gritz, except for events such as the Oklahoma City Gun and Knife Show, seems to be taking a decidedly low profile in regard to militia activities these days.

Samuel Sherwood (Militia-style White Nationalist)

Samuel Sherwood once headed the United States Militia Association (USMA) based in Blackfoot, ID. He was involved in 1995 in organizing popular opposition to an environmentalist-backed legal injunction issued by federal judge David Ezra of Hawaii. The injunction was feared as a first step toward shutting down mining and other extraction activities in five national forests in Idaho in order to protect endangered species. At meetings in Challis, ID, Sherwood advised that if the forests were actually shut down (the court ultimately left the forests open, requiring all parties to work out a compromise to protect the river salmon) that Idaho citizens should "get a semi-automatic assault rifle . . . ," among other things. He tried to enlist people in his militia cause so as to fight "the green Gestapo" of federal agents and environmentalists (Stern 1997, 129).

In 1992 Sherwood wrote a book, *The Little Republics,* in which he outlined a "political war" with Satan, which would destroy the nation, necessitating a rebirth. Post-war America would bring about some significant Sherwood-style changes including execution of homosexuals, abortionists, rapists, and disloyal politicians; and an end to income taxes, Social Security, the DEA, BATF, the Departments of Labor, HHS, and Energy; and, oddly enough, an end to marriage licenses (Stern 1997, 166).

Sherwood has made threats of violence to Idaho legislators who sell out to the demands of the federal government (see Chapter II for explanation). In 1996 he began, with modest success, a political action committee called the "Liberty of Conscience" to raise money to contribute to the election of politicians sympathetic to militia causes. Sherwood's lack of legislator support in Idaho and his inability to raise much money through his Liberty of Conscience PAC showed that he had far less clout than he often indicated when claiming that his militia group had 5,000 members from 12 states. Failures and problems for Sherwood's pet election initiatives concerning abortion, legal recognition of militias, and religious issues proved that most Idaho voters viewed him as "a loose cannon" (see Dan Yurman, "Idaho's Plutonian Landscape," *The Progressive Populist, Internet Edition,* January 1996). Most recently, Sherwood has left Idaho for Utah and the leadership of the USMA and its organizational structure have become inoperative.

Jared Taylor (White Nationalist)

Jared Taylor is head of the American Renaissance movement and editor of its publication of the same name, centered in Fairfax County, VA. Taylor attempts to take an intellectual approach to the issues of demographic change, immigration and race in America. However, he is consistently white nationalist in his perspectives and conclusions.

At a 1996 conference on race and immigration in Louisville, KY, Taylor hit upon the familiar white nationalist theme that whites were steadily becoming the racial minority in the country. As Taylor argued, the effects of such a population change are significant. ". . . [W]hites will withdraw from more and more parts of the United States. It will be *physically possible* for them to live with the Mexicans . . . or the blacks . . ., but whites will do just about anything to avoid it" (Jared Taylor, "Race and Nation: a speech at the 1996 *AR* Conference," [Internet] May 1996, Louisville, KY).

Taylor is a defender of racial separation and of the view that many racial minorities are genetically and biologically programmed to have a lower IQ than Euro-Caucasian people. Part of the 1996 Conference dealt with issues of race and IQ ("1996 AR Conference a Huge Success," *Stalking the Wild Taboo—Latest news, Internet,* May 1996, www.amren.com/conf.96htm).

Further, Jared Taylor favors racial/ethnic separation even when IQ, performance or behavioral standards fall to the favor of a minority over whites, as is true of many in the Asian community. Taylor has asserted that even though some, such Japanese or Chinese immigrants and descendants, are productive in their communities and are even, to some degree, "superior" to European descendants, they are still *different* (Taylor's emphasis). The bottom line for Taylor is that whites will leave a community once it becomes predominantly Asian, even though Asians are law abiding and have high IQs, because the lifestyle and culture of the community is forever changed and is no longer their own—the white majority's ("Race and Nation," [Internet] May 1996, Louisville, KY).

Taylor hopes to use his organizations, publications, conferences, and forums to wake up the sleeping white majority from either its apathy or "guilt." America, for him, is a country intended for white Europeans. While minorities may be entitled to their own countries somewhere and somehow, they are not entitled to the America Taylor and the embattled white majority have always known.

Richard Girnt Butler (Neo-Nazi, White Nationalist)

Richard Girnt Butler was born in Colorado in 1918 and moved with his family to California as a teenager. A trained engineer, Butler worked in the aircraft industry in California. It was there in 1962 that he came into contact with the likes of Col. William Potter Gale, who was associated with the revival of the radical, often aggressive, Posse Comitatus, and came into contact also with the Rev. Wesley Swift, an ordained Methodist minister, who directed the Church of Jesus Christ Christian in Hollywood, CA. Swift was influenced by and in turn defended the racist pastor/orator of the World War II era, Gerald L. K. Smith (Bushart, Craig and Barnes, 1998, 192).

According to Butler's own statements as recounted by Professor James Aho (1990, 55), meeting Swift had a most telling impact on Butler's own life and political future. Swift preached the doctrine of fundamental Christian Identity, a racialist perspective of the

Bible which sees white, Western European peoples as the only truly civilized and "holy" chosen children of God.

Butler was, along with Swift and others, involved with the organization of the California Christian Defense League in response to the fears of Soviet communism in the early 1960s. Ordained as an Identity minister after completing a correspondence program of Biblical study, Butler took over Swift's church upon the death of his mentor. By the mid-1970s, Butler had relocated to a paramilitary-type compound near Hayden Lake in the mountains of Northern Idaho. There he established the Aryan Nations as the political arm of his Church of Jesus Christ Christian and advocated Nazi-style flags, uniforms, discipline, and paramilitary training (Bushart, Craig and Barnes, 1998, 193).

Butler's group holds an annual Aryan World Congress in northern Idaho (and planned to do so again in July 2001 despite the group's recent legal/financial losses) which attracts neo-Nazis, Klansmen, Identity worshipers, militia types, and various other radical, white nationalists. Various members of the terrorist group The Order were once affiliated with or frequent visitors to Butler's racialist compound. Such include Robert Matthews (who died in a shootout with the FBI), Bruce Pierce (convicted of killing Denver radio personality Alan Berg in 1984), Gary Yarborough (a militia man convicted on weapons and racketeering charges, as well as assaulting an FBI agent in a drive-by shooting), and David Lane (a Klansman convicted of involvement in the Berg murder and of racketeering and conspiracy) (Flynn and Gerhardt, 1989).

Butler, along with others, was indicted and tried on sedition charges in federal court in 1988, but he and other defendants were acquitted (George and Wilcox, 1996, 341). Butler operates a successful recruitment program through an active prison ministry, through publications, and through Internet homepages. Although law enforcement investigations and monitoring, internal controversy over money and tactics, and heightened public awareness due to the violence associated with former members have served to diminish the numbers and prominence at Butler's World Congresses, the Aryan Nations pastor remains an influential force in racialist and anti-government politics. He remains a sort of "Godfather" to many in racial extremism. Recently, Butler and his organization suffered a most serious legal blow stemming from a $6 million judgment against Butler; the Aryan Nations; Saphire,

Inc. (Butler's front company for owning Aryan Nations' properties); the Aryan Nations' Director of Security; another security employee at Butler's compound; and three unidentified Nations' members. The civil suit resulted from an incident in July 1998 when Idaho area resident Victoria Keenan and her son Jason, a resident of Washington state, were alleged to have been assaulted by gunfire and physical force as the Aryan Nations security people shot their car, forced them to crash on a public road, and proceeded to physically assault and threaten the two citizens. The incident originated apparently in the fact that Victoria, a resident of Bonner County, ID, who often uses the public road near the Aryan Nations compound, had stopped her car in front of the compound's entrance so that Jason might retrieve a wallet he had lost out of the car. Upon leaving the area, Keenan's car backfired, which was apparently the spark which set off the Aryan Nations' security forces on their spree (*Southern Poverty Law Center, Internet.*" Law Center Information: Legal Action," updated 3 June 1999).

The Southern Poverty Law Center (SPLC), based in Montgomery, AL, committed to the suit and has had many notable successes in the past in crippling such hate groups as the Klan through civil awards of financial damages to their clients, who have been victims of hate activity. While Butler has put in place a chain of command and has essentially appointed as his successor the anti-Semitic preacher Neuman Britton ("Neuman Britton," *ADL [Anti Defamation League] Backgrounder Internet.* 20 July 1998, accessed 3 June 1999), his difficulties are mounting. Butler himself apparently scuffled with local law enforcement personnel shortly before the Keenan incident as the officers were attempting to make lawful arrests at the neo-Nazi compound (*Southern Poverty Law Center, Internet.* 3 June 1999). Butler also felt constrained to drop a countersuit against the SPLC in the Keenan case on May 28, 1999. (There was some indication from a previous Aryan Nations website that Butler could not find enough attorneys in the northwest region to take on his cause to do effective battle with SPLC; *www.nidlink.com/%7earyanvic/lawsuit.html,* updated 20 April 1999). As a result of the judgment against them in the Keenan case, Aryan Nations has recently had to forfeit their property near Hayden Lake, ID, and reorganize some operations to California.

Ultimately, the victorious Keenans were awarded the Aryan Nations compound as part of the court settlement. The property was then purchased by human rights activist and millionaire Greg Carr, of the Harvard Institute on Human Rights. Original plans were for Carr, working with the Kootenai County, ID, Task Force on Human Rights, to establish a nonprofit, human rights educational center at the site. Carr's wealth was established through Internet businesses and he seeks to promote human rights issues throughout the country (phone interview with Leslie Goddard, Director of Idaho Human Rights Commission of Boise, ID, 16 May 2001). Recent news reports from Kootenai County, ID, and Spokane, WA, have provided multiple indications that Carr has determined (as of May 18, 2001) to have the buildings at the compound burned for a fire training exercise by local firefighters and to build anew rather than renovate the existing structures. Richard Butler, still apparently residing in Kootenai County, is said to be pleased that his former headquarters will be torched rather than used by human rights activists.

Pete Peters (Christian Identity Religious Leader)

Pete Peters is pastor of the Laporte, CO, Church of Christ, a Christian Identity Church. As a young minister he served as an associate pastor in Gering, NE, where he helped to influence a number of parishioners in the Identity doctrine of British Israelism (Aho 1990, 202). He continues to advocate this same theology today with even greater impact through his sizable congregation and his shortwave radio, tape, and Internet ministries offered under the rubric of "Scriptures for America."

Basically, Christian Identity and the underlying theology of British Israelism contend that the holy nation of ancient Israel was destroyed both before and after the coming of Jesus Christ in Palestine and was scattered in a desperate fashion. The "lost tribes" and "true Jews" (according to the Christian Identity teachers) migrated across mountains, plains, and seas to Central and Western Europe, ending up in important respects in Great Britain and even Ireland. Thus, the holy nation remnant of today is of necessity European, and in major parts, Anglo-Saxon.

Peters perpetuates and elaborates upon this doctrine of British Israelism, often with racist overtones, in his online newsletter, *Scriptures for America: Worldwide*. This Internet publication is very professionally done, organized, and colorful. Peters' congregation sponsors numerous, and apparently popular, events—such as a Rocky Mountain Family Camp. In his newsletter Peters frequently rails against the media, public opinion, black helicopters, the UN, the New World Order, and of course, the Jews and their alleged conspiracies in politics and world finance (Pete Peters, "Armed and Dangerous—With Faith, Hope and Love," *Scriptures for America: Worldwide online,* 4(1997), 21 February 1998, 1-2). The Christian Identity group offers a virtual one-stop shopping opportunity for the faithful, featuring even a Long Distance Calling Card for sale, along with the usual religious and political books and tracts (from Aho, research files, 28 April 1999).

John Trochmann (Militia Leader)

John Trochmann is co-founder and political leader of the Militia of Montana based in Noxon, MT. The Militia of Montana Home Page provides the viewer with the opportunity to access background information on Trochmann. In general, one finds by accessing Trochmann's biographical sketch that the militia leader was brought up in Minnesota on a cattle and grain farm. He served in the Naval Air Force in the '60s and received an honorable discharge in 1965. Trochmann and his two brothers operated a highly successful business making snowmobile parts and accessories for sale all across North America. Selling his share in the business and other ventures, Trochmann moved to northwestern Montana in the early 1980s. Though in semi-retirement, John was a supporter of the patriot/militia movement and was incensed and energized by the federal dispute with the Randy Weaver family. In 1994 he helped to found the Militia of Montana (*Militia of Montana Home Page,* updated 7 May 1997, 1-2).

Seeing itself as a true citizen's militia in contrast to the corrupted, federally dominated National Guard, Trochmann's Montana group avows from its web page that it, ". . . is an educational organization dedicated to the preservation of the freedoms of ALL citizens of the State of Montana and of the United States of America" (*Militia of Montana Page,* 1 April 1999, 1). Further, the web page argues that the National Guard's weapons, equipment and entire operation are owned and controlled by the feds, in clear violation, as the Militia of Montana sees it, of the Second Amendment of the U.S. Constitution.[1]

John Trochmann was arrested in 1995, along with several of the Montana "freemen," on charges involving alleged intimidation and weapons carrying. Upon an investigation of the Montana attorney general's office, however, all felony charges and all but two lesser charges were dismissed (George and Wilcox 1996, 262).

Trochmann carries on extensive militia educational and entrepreneurial efforts. He markets many books, videos and audio tapes on militia and anti-government concerns. Furthermore, Trochmann lectures to universities and high schools in the western states, and, occasionally, elsewhere. For instance, Trochmann has lectured to students at Yale and at the University of Tennessee, Knoxville.

Although an active militia leader and one who is absorbed by fears of a supposed UN, one-world conspiracy to dismantle American constitutional government, Trochmann has repeatedly and publicly denied that he is racist or supportive of racist groups. He has become a kind of "elder statesman" for the American militia movement; he is apparently an effective public speaker, whose baritone voice and documentary style often serve to sanitize his militant message for young listeners.

James J. (J.J.) Johnson
(Ex-militia Leader? Radical Libertarian-Patriot)

James J. (J.J.) Johnson is a former utility company worker who helped to found the Ohio Unorganized Militia. An African American, Johnson received a good deal of public attention when he, along with others such as Norm Olson of Michigan and Bob Fletcher of Montana, testified before the U.S. Senate in 1995 after the Oklahoma City bombing (Ed Vogel, "Militia movement figure moves to Vegas," *Las Vegas Review-Journal, Online,* 17 November 1997). Interestingly enough, in May 1997 Johnson and his wife, attorney/physician Nancy Lord, moved to Las Vegas, NV, whereupon Johnson indicated that he had severed all ties with the militia. Johnson now apparently works as an investigator in his wife's law firm. His wife Nancy was the 1992 Libertarian Party nominee for vice-president. Lord is said to represent a number of "patriot" (anti-government) leaders. Johnson has something of a running verbal feud with the Southern Poverty Law Center of Montgomery, AL.

Mark Potok, of the Southern Poverty Law Center, has said that Johnson has not left behind his violence-baiting days. Johnson has allegedly made inciteful statements, for instance, calling for a street in New Hampshire to be named after Carl Drega, who killed a judge, two police officers and a weekly newspaper editor in August of 1997 and was then killed by the police. Johnson has claimed that his remarks were taken out of context; that the Southern Poverty Law Center's existence is testament to the passivity and nonviolence of patriots; that the Center itself has practiced racism and discrimination against its employees (Vogel, 17 November 1997, 1-2).

Whatever his current status in the militia movement, it can be said with credibility that Johnson remains an important anti-government "patriot." He finds that most, if not all, of what the federal officials and lawmakers are doing today is repugnant and adverse to the ideals of the Constitution. He remains politically ambitious, tinkering with the possibility of running for the local sheriff's position in Nevada and meddling in the governor's contest in his new state (Vogel, 17 November 1997, 2).

Linda Thompson (Influential Militia Advocate)

Linda Thompson is a leader of the Unorganized Militia and the American Justice Federation. Thompson, from Indianapolis, IN, has created significant controversy in and out of the militia movement in the United States. In 1994 she called for an armed militia march on Washington, D.C. Such a position brought great opposition from other militia leaders who considered the notion utterly foolish at best. Thompson ultimately called off the protest due to a lack of support (Ken McVay, "ADL Report: Armed and Dangerous: Indiana," *Internet* 21 August, 1996). Thompson has produced two videos on the Waco, TX, incident, arguing that the siege was part of a general government conspiracy. Patriot groups and members seem to find these videos compelling, but overall, Thompson's influence in the national militia movement has declined. She still garners support through her Internet contacts ("Prominent Patriots list," *Southern Poverty Law Center Militia Task Force, Internet,* 22 July, 1998).

The libertarian Internet publication *Revolution* describes Thompson as a sarcastic, somewhat erratic character given to public pronouncements that are used to stimulate public attention more than anything else (29 July 1998). The iconoclastic Internet publication *DCI* (Digital Culture Interactive) *News* describes Linda Thompson as a militia/patriot activist with a penchant for conspiracy theories involving a UN-style takeover of the United States by force, and the resulting domination and subjugation of our citizens by the UN military and "New World Order" bureaucrats ("Militia/Patriot Movement," *DCI News,* 29 July, 1998).

Notes

1. For a thorough and effective treatment of the history and development of the National Guard and the Military Reserve see Gary Hart, *The Minuteman: Restoring An Army of the People,* 1998. New York: Free Press. This work covers the development of federal laws regarding the Guard and federal/state relationships pertaining thereto, starting with the Militia Act (1903), which essentially attached greater importance to the Guard and the National Defense Act of 1920, which established the force structure of regulars, reserves and Guard operating today. Hart also clarifies, in contrast to the views of groups such as the Militia of Montana, that George Washington himself indicated in 1783 that the state citizen militia be under national control and have uniform training and organizational standards (98-99). Further, Hart indicates (153) that the readiness of the citizen-soldiers would properly be the responsibility of their officers, with the supervision of regular units as Hart believes is foreseen in Art. I, section 8, paragraph 16 of the Constitution of the United States, which reads that Congress has the power "To provide for organizing, arming, and disciplining the Militia, and for governing such Part of them as may be employed in the in the Service of the United States, reserving to the States respectively, the appointment of Officers, and the Authority of training the Militia according to the discipline prescribed by Congress."

Chapter Discussion Questions

(Chapter III—Recent Terrorist Events and Social
and Political Responses and Chapter IV—Profiles in Anger)

1. Identify and elaborate upon several of the social/political system problems in America today which seem to be associated with or reflected in right-wing extremism or terrorism.

2. How serious a problem is the incidence of hate crimes in the United States? Describe and explain. What role does racism play in these crimes?

3. In your view, why are Americans generally so negative in their evaluation of the following?

   a. Government officials

   b. Government agencies

4. Discuss the costs and impact on individuals, government, and society of the Oklahoma City Bombing. (Focus on attitudes, dollars, laws and lives.)

5. Briefly, explain the relationship between each of the items below and extremism or terrorism.

   a. *The Turner Diaries*

   b. The use of the Internet

   c. Branch Davidians

   d. Richard Butler

   e. The Order

   f. Bo Gritz

   g. Richard McLaren

6. Discuss the philosophical connections between the Sagebrush Rebellion and Anti-property Tax Movements of the 1970s and militia activists such as the militia of Montana today.

Suggestions for Further Reading

Ashby, LeRoy and Rod Gramer. 1994. *Fighting the Odds: The Life of Senator Frank Church.* Pullman, WA: Washington State University.

Daily Oklahoman. 1995. 19 May.

Macdonald, Andrew. (Pseud. For William L. Pierce). 1985. *The Turner Diaries.* Arlington, VA: Nat'l Vanguard books.

Sears, David O. And Jack Citrin. 1986. "Tax Revolt: Proposition 13 in California and Its Aftermath." In *Bureaucratic Power in National Policy Making,* 4th edition. Ed. Francis E. Rourke. Boston: Little, Brown and Co.

Southern Poverty Law Center, Internet. 1998. *Intelligence Report.* Spring and Winter issues.

Wilson, James Q. 1986. "The Rise of the Bureaucratic State." In *Bureaucratic Power in National Policy Making,* 4th edition. Ed. Francis E. Rourke. Boston: Little, Brown and Co.

CHAPTER V

System Response

"To make anyone answerable for doing evil to others is the rule; to make him answerable for not preventing evil is, comparatively speaking, the exception."
—John Stuart Mill. 1859. *On Liberty* ("Introductory").

"Policymaking is a process of interaction among governmental and nongovernmental actors, policy is the outcome of that interaction."
—Randall B. Ripley and Grace A. Franklin. 1984.
Congress, the Bureaucracy, and Public Policy, Third Edition
Homewood, IL: Dorsey, 1.

The rather patchwork and reactive nature of the American political system's response to terrorist activity in the 1990s is illustrated by the varied and spasmodic efforts of the legislative and executive branches of the federal government. To make policy even more difficult to coordinate and implement, there is a plethora of different agencies at each level of government (federal, state and local) with fractional but important responsibilities for combating terrorism directed at Americans.

Since American concerns for terrorism in the Cold War era revolved around international sources and actions, the U.S. Department of State traditionally took the lead in directing the political system's response to terrorism. J. Brent Wilson has shown that the State Department today divides terrorism efforts into three categories. First, a Department Committee, the Policy Coordinating Committee on Terrorism, conducts policy oversight and management of terrorism issues. In addition, a crisis management group within the Department oversees response to a specific terrorist event through the creation of a task force that would also maintain contact with crisis teams at the White House, Pentagon and intelligence agencies. Third, State contributes to specially trained counterterrorism teams that assist both embassies and foreign governments in responding to international terrorism (1994, 178-179).

In order to illustrate the incremental, reactive nature of the federal policy toward terrorism we present a chronological catalog of federal terrorist policies from 1970 to the present. The reader will note that policies are often fashioned in reaction to events, and not in anticipation of them. Also, the policies, until very recently, were directed toward responding to the traditional, international style of terrorism, typified by Middle Eastern or European ideological groups. Domestic terror, random domestic threats of terrorism, as well as chemical/biological threats went unrecognized, for the most part, until the 1990s. Further, the National Security Council, the State Department, and the FBI, traditional political/bureaucratic organizations, have historically been given the major responsibilities for coordination and networking of federal counterterrorist efforts. After the catalog of policies, we will briefly consider whether it is a good idea, in light of the acts and threats of terror by American extremists, to continue to operate according to current bureaucratic and political practices in response to domestic terrorism.

Catalog of Government Policies Against Terrorism:

[From J. Brent Wilson. 1994. "The United States Response to International Terrorism," The Deadly Sin of Terrorism, ed. David A. Charters. Westport, CT: Greenwood Press. Items were adapted from listings in Wilson unless otherwise designated by separate source.]

1970   FAA activated in response to PFLP hijackings. Nixon created Federal Sky Marshal program, putting U.S. Marshals on international flights. Program formally terminated in 1974.

1972   Cabinet Committee to Combat Terrorism set up after Munich Olympics massacre in September. Coordinated interagency actions to combat terrorism.

1977 Carter separates crisis response from policy development
and coordination. Crisis management given to Special
Coordination Committee of the National Security Council;
lead agencies to be designated for policy coordination
depending on the event—State Department for international; FAA for airline incidents; Justice and FBI for
domestic troubles; NSC for settling interagency disputes.
Long-range planning, operations coordination, and interagency communication given to Executive Committee on
Terrorism (ECT), with representatives from State, Defense,
Justice, Treasury, Transportation, Energy, CIA, and NSC.

1982 Secretary of State Haig and President Reagan replace ECT
with an Interdepartmental Group on Terrorism (IGT);
membership was expanded from that of ECT to include
vice president and the DEA. Lead agency for counter
international threats was still Department of State.
Reorganization and expansion of Office for Combating
Terrorism (OCT), which had been created in 1976. New
director given ambassadorial rank.

1984 OCT adds Emergency Planning and expands further to
include coordination of intelligence, administration of
Anti-Terrorism Assistance Program, and ensuring ade-
quacy of emergency response plans at overseas missions.

*[From "International Terrorism: American Hostages," U.S. Dept.
of State (Office of the Coordinator for Counterterrorism) 17
October 1995]*

1984 October 1984 enactment of 18 USC 1203 (Act for
Prevention and Punishment of the Crime of Hostage-
Taking). Law implements UN Convention On Hostage-
taking of December 1979, providing that seizure of a U.S.
national as a hostage anywhere in the world is a crime, as
is any hostage-taking action in which the U.S. government
is a target or the perpetrator is a U.S. national. Actions by
private persons or entities that have the effect of aiding
and abetting the hostage-taking, concealing knowledge of
it from authorities, or obstructing its investigation may
themselves be in violation of U.S. law.

1985 New Bureau of Diplomatic Security and Office of Ambassador-at-large for Counterterrorism.

1989 State Department's tri-level counterterrorist effort: 1) Policy Coordinating Committee on Terrorism; 2) Crisis Management task forces in lead agencies—State, Defense, CIA and White House; 3) Response teams to assist embassies and foreign governments.

1993 Clinton commences wholesale reorganization at State; Bureau of Narcotics, Terrorism and crime takes over counterterrorism resonsibilities of Bureau of Diplomatic Security and counterterrorism coordinator made Deputy Assistant Secretary of State. [Distinction between ordinary organized crime and political crime had become blurred.]

[From Lois Ember, Chemical and Engineering News, 4 November 1996, 11]

1995 Presidential Decision Directive 39—(PDD39)—U.S. Policy on Counterterrorism laid out, generally. FBI given lead responsibility for managing a crisis posed by a credible threat of deployment of a weapon of mass destruction. Federal Emergency Management Agency (FEMA) to take the lead in managing consequences of terrorists' mass weapon usage

[From "Counterterrorism," Office of the White House Press Secretary 30 April 1996 and "Chapter VI: Legal Issues Pertaining to Victims of Terrorism," Office for Victims of Crime Resource Center—Responding to Terrorism Victims: Oklahoma City and Beyond October 2000; www.ojpusdog.gov/ove/infors/respterrorism/chap6.html)]

1996 April 24, 1996, the President signed S. 735—Antiterrorism and Effective Death Penalty Act—included proposals giving law enforcement officials new tools to stop terrorists before a strike and to bring them to justice after a strike. Bans fund raising in the U.S. that supports terrorist organizations; allows U.S. to deport known terrorists from American soil without being compelled by the terrorists to divulge classified information. Terrorists barred from

entering the U.S. Amended the Victims of Crime Act
(VOCA) by adding 42 USC 19693(b) to allow the Office
of Victims of Crime (OVC) access to emergency reserve
funds in both domestic and international terrorist incidents.

*[From "Implementations of the 25 Recommendations from the
Paris Ministerial," U.S. Dept. of State (Office of the Coordinator
for Counterterrorism) 11 December 1997]*

1996 Comprehensive revision of Immigration and Nationality
Act strengthens ability of U.S. Immigration officials to
exclude and deport individuals suspected of terrorist activities

1997 Comprehensive implementation of the 265 recommendations of the July 1996 Paris Terrorism Ministerial
Conference of the nations of the P-8 (Political 8) industrial,
democratic world powers. Implementation included administrative actions, executive orders, financial supplements to
existing budgets, legal enforcements, legal implementations, and policy coordination along a variety of fronts.
These efforts were devoted to improving legal cooperation and capability; deterrence, prosecution, and punich-
ment of terrorists; improved control over asylum, border
and travel document issues; ratification of international
agreements; bans and penalties on terrorist fund raising;
and improving information exchange on terrorism.

2001 President George W. Bush declares a "War on Terrorism"
in response to terrorist attacks on New York City and
Washington, D.C. on September 11, 2001. Federal/state
efforts made to enhance domestic security. Air strikes
against terrorist targets in Afghanistan begin in October.

In terms of evaluation and assessment of government policies
on counterterrorism, we make several observations. First, we would
agree in the essentials with Wilson's characterization of policies of
the '70s and '80s and argue that his characterization of the policies
devoted to international terrorism of these earlier decades is also
indicative of the policies of the '90s devoted to domestic instances
of terror. Policy tends to be overly bureaucratic in nature, with faulty
and haphazard interagency cooperation. Policymakers tend to focus

on short-term quick fixes to try to get immediate results and to pla-
cate an impatient and fearful populace. While this may produce
short-run political gains, it is often ineffective in terms of strategy
for combating and preventing terrorist acts. Policymakers and citizens alike tend to couch efforts to combat terrorism in military war-
fare terms (Wilson 1994, 202). Thus, overemphasis is given to solutions to terrorism which involve significant deployment of military
hardware, technology, and surveillance. Flexible, maneuverable
responses are overlooked. Education, training, negotiation, diplomacy, and patience are not emphasized enough. These sentiments
have been echoed by the Honorable Morris D. Busby, the former
U.S. Ambassador to Columbia (1991-1993) and Coordinator for
Counterterrorism (1989-91), in his testimony before the U.S. Senate
Permanent Subcommittee on Investigations/ Committee on
Government Affairs on March 27, 1996. Busby stressed the need for
better information collection and analysis and more effective monitoring, tracking and preemption of terrorist group activity. The former ambassador asserted that the bedrock principles which guide
our approach to international terrorism,[1] must also inform the
national effort versus domestic terrorists (1996, 2). The lead domestic terrorist-fighting agency, the FBI, needs to devote more attention
and manpower to the analysis of case reports for strategic analysis
to prepare better for new developments and future problems with
troublesome groups (Busby 1996).

Furthermore, Busby (1996) pointed to deficiencies in interagency coordination, planning and readiness to respond to domestic terrorism, particularly as threats require action from multiple
agencies across federal, state and local levels of government.

In looking at the chronology of government policies toward terrorism since the 1970s, we might make better overall sense of what
has happened by use of what the authors call a Reactionary-
Incrementalist Model of Counterterrorism Policy (See Figure 4.1).

According to this descriptive model, the policy process is begun
by a triggering event, such as a bombing, highjacking, or assassination. The triggering event[2] creates the demand and the support for
a governmental response.

This response is reactive in nature, and policy strategy, decisions and tactics are developed as policymakers move along,
responding to the crisis or triggering event. The reaction changes,
usually, as the policymakers learn more and as an event fully

unfolds. Refinements, additions and subtractions to previous policy are made during the crisis. Once the triggering event has been significantly responded to by government policy, policymakers and citizens begin to judge the success or failure of the government's reaction. Generally, the reaction brings mixed reviews or results. In any event, policy reassessment then invariably takes place, with subsequent changes in the reaction, as well as long-term demands for new proposals or policies which would more effectively prevent or combat future triggering events like the initial one.

Long-term proposals, especially laws, have a way of impacting the sociopolitical environment so as to create new conditions for extremist action and government reaction, and the cycle repeats itself. Policy towards terrorism is, therefore, reactive and indeed

FIGURE 4.1

**REACTIONARY-INCREMENTALIST
MODEL OF COUNTERTERRORISM POLICY***

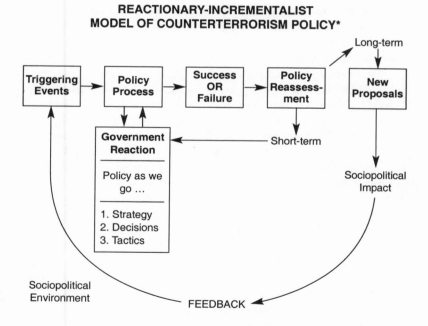

* This model uses the systems framework for the analysis of social and political problems most popularly developed by David Easton (1971) in the field of international politics.

pushed and pulled by events. Our chronology of policy developments presented earlier in this chapter illustrates the fits and starts
of policy-making. Policy is also incremental: small changes are
made as government agents struggle to manage unfolding events so
as to minimize damage to the society and the government's own
credibility.[3] These changes tend to be in the direction of the already
known, already tried, or already politically acceptable solutions.
This approach is true of incremental policymaking in general.
Further, the known, tried and acceptable solutions are invariably, as
Wilson has argued, military-like, with emphasis on using heavy
firepower and sophisticated weapons and technology, with a heavy
reliance on electronic surveillance methods for information. The
problem with these status quo acceptable solutions is that the terrorist events don't often lend themselves to the known, tried and
politically acceptable.

An example or mini-case study of one such triggering event will
illustrate the pitfalls of Reactionary-Incrementalist policymaking.
One among a number of examples of counterterrorism policy of the
reactionary-incrementalist kind is the federal response to the activities of the Weaver family at Ruby Ridge, ID, in August 1992.
Though not engaged in a large-scale anti-government action at the
time counterterrorist policies were triggered, Weaver was alleged
to have sold several illegal guns to an informer for the Bureau of
Alcohol, Tobacco and Firearms (Bennett 1995, 448). Further,
Weaver was associated with extremist, racist and right-wing groups
(Stern 1997, 19-27 and Baradat 1997, 285). The government pursued a traditional law enforcement approach trying to bring Weaver
to court, and when he failed to appear, sent the proper authorities
to apprehend the suspected arms dealer. Bad feeling between
Weaver and the government had been building for over a year as
letters from his wife Vicky to the U.S. District Attorney's office
indicate (Baradat 1997, 283). When the marshals arrived to sur-
veil the mountain-top area in line with traditional police tactics,
an armed confrontation ensued. Weaver's resistance and the authorities' pursuit resulted in gunfire and the death of a federal deputy
marshal (Bennett 1995, 448). The Weavers, in turn, lost their 14-
year-old son Sam in the initial shooting.

Having encountered greater difficulty in making the arrest than
anticipated and having now lost a decorated and honorable marshal,
the government, as well as the media and attentive public, judged

the initial, traditional effort as essentially a failure. Local residents and militia and other extremist groups rallied in support of the Weavers, often protesting and picketing law enforcement personnel at roadblocks established near the Weaver cabin (Stern 1997, 24-26).

The FBI and other authorities then reassessed the initial policy. In the short term this reevaluation resulted not in an abandonment or suspension of traditional law enforcement methods, but in an incremental adjustment or increase in the policy. In sum, more manpower, more firepower, and a freer rein for agents to respond to the Weavers with lethal force were measures put in place. Standing operational plans and policies of the Hostage Rescue Team at Ruby Ridge were ignored in order that the agents on site be allowed to shoot at their individual discretion, and not necessarily in self-defense. Although confusion surrounded the bureaucratic flow of information between Washington, D.C., and Idaho, orders were apparently given to heighten the flexibility of response of the field operatives at Ruby Ridge (Bennett 1995, 449).

The dramatic results of the policy reassessment and the added tactical flexibility of the authorities illustrate the real pitfalls associated with reactionary-incrementalist policies toward terrorist activity. Mrs. Weaver was killed by authorities in the subsequent siege of the Weaver home. Weaver, himself wounded, ultimately surrendered, as did a young associate named Harris.

Subsequent to the Weaver shootings and the media and governmental investigations of them, the FBI and other political institutions undertook a more long-term reassessment of federal policy. FBI Director Freeh gave reprimands to a dozen employees connected to the siege. Also, the Director suspended Larry Potts, former head of the FBI's criminal division, for his work in relation to the incidents in Idaho (Bennett 1995, 449). Weaver received a $3.1 million dollar settlement from the government for the wrongful deaths of his wife and son (Stern 1997, 39). Weaver was also acquitted by a jury trial of murder in the death of the federal deputy. Senate hearings were held, resulting in further negative publicity for the FBI and federal law enforcement agencies. Embarrassment was plentiful.

The sociopolitical impact of Weaver's operations and federal efforts to respond to them can be seen in the outcry and further paranoia of militia groups in the country. Further, the agents of the federal government were even more determined to implement traditional apprehension and arrest tactics when faced with the stock-piling of illegal weapons by the Branch Davidian sect in Waco, TX, in 1993. As Bennett (1995, 449) indicates, federal authorities, particularly the ATF, were unwilling to "wait out" Koresh and his followers in light of the shooting of the federal marshal at Ruby Ridge. Despite the tenuous logic behind the ATF's initial attempt to raid the Waco compound, skepticism in negotiation or in attempts to arrest Koresh after the Davidians had settled in the compound blinded the federal authorities in the pursuit of the group.

The federal government's final, destructive assault on the Waco compound led to a heightened paranoia on the part of militia groups and right-wing extremists. Timothy McVeigh, one of a number of militia-style sympathizers or participants who kept vigil at the site of the Waco confrontation, was said to be incensed beyond toler-ance at the feds' attack on the Davidians (Stickney 1996, 154-155, 165). As a result of the events at Waco and Ruby Ridge, militia groups prepared for what they saw as an all-out war on their con-stitutional rights, particularly Second Amendment rights. Baradat (1997) has shown how militia leaders threatened U.S. Senators in testimony before Congress, warned of thousands of Gurkha troops poised in northern Michigan and about to attack the Midwest upon order of the UN, and argued that the feds were controlled by Satanic forces. All of this was coincident with warnings that Ruby Ridge and Waco indicated that violent confrontation between cit-izens and the federal government was imminent (Baradat 1997, 162). The long-term effects of the flexible fire and return fire pol-icy of the federal officials at Ruby Ridge have been of tremendous consequence when seen in line with similar decisions to up the ante of traditional law enforcement tactics at Waco. The Oklahoma City catastrophe of 1995 proceeded from the climate resulting from Waco in 1993 and Ruby Ridge in 1992.

The Reactionary-Incrementalist model of counterterrorism pol-icy may, therefore, be illustrated in a case scenario by Figure 4.2, which is focused upon the Ruby Ridge incident.

Having illustrated the reactionary-incrementalist nature of fed-eral counterterrorist policies and the pitfalls of such policies, we now turn our attention to an overview of federal, state and local relations in responding to terrorism on the domestic front. Also, we will address the general nature of federal solutions to terrorist threats or incidents, with a focus on current institutional and tradi-

FIGURE 4.2

RUBY RIDGE

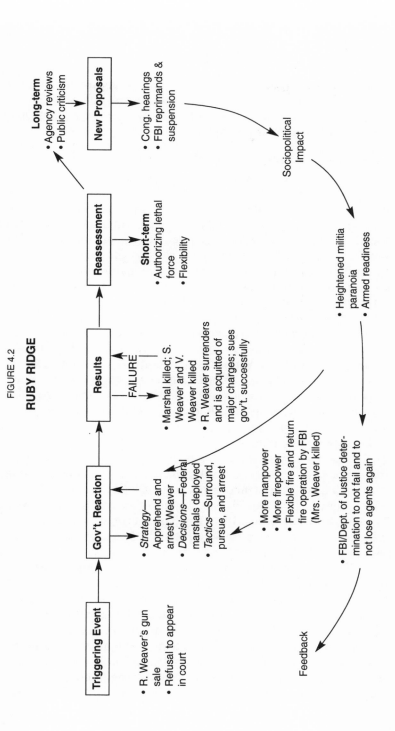

tional law enforcement policies. Finally, we will assess some of
the aspects of a more effective counter-terrorist policy which are
presently lacking. The next section, then, will be more philosophical than the section just completed.

Federal-State Policies—the Rule in the U.S.

America, as a country, is politically unique in many ways, not
the least of which is an adherence to federalism as a system of
government. From Madison's stealthy crafting of the Tenth Amendment of the U.S. Constitution, through the anguish of attempted
secession and Civil War, the enlargement of national power following economic depression and world war, the zeal of the Great
Society, and up to the retrenchment of national power of the present day, the American political system has struck a constant though
turbulent balance of responsibility between federal and state
government.

America's tendency to place state governments at the vital center of critical areas of policy-making is surprising if one examines
the propensity of other democracies for unitary systems with strong
central government (e.g., United Kingdom, France, and Sweden).
Education, transportation and law enforcement are among key policy areas which have historically been directed through state action,
and still are in large part.

Legal policies outlining responses to terrorism represent another
important area of political action over which states exercise many
critical powers. Twenty-five states have specific statutes dealing
with terrorism. These statutes range from laws such as Minnesota's,
which punish terroristic threats, to those laws as found in West
Virginia, which treat terrorist acts as typical criminal conduct under
criminal statutes (Smith 1994, appendix.). The tendency for state
responses to terrorism has been to try to cover terrorist acts under
the criminal code and to look at such acts, in terms of enforcement, as nonextraordinary crimes against the public. State policy
therefore stresses traditional law enforcement strategies. Emphasis
is on reaction and response rather than detection and prevention.
The way to more effective police response has been seen, until the
recent surge in community policing, to be through more manpower,
more and improved firepower, and advances in law enforcement
technology, including widespread applications of electronic surveillance. Personalized law enforcement detection and network-

ing have taken hold in one area of policing since the late 1970s as communities were increasingly forced to deal with high volume narcotics trafficking. Given the need to get "into the minds" more and behind the scenes of the militias to discern their motivation, agents Duffy and Brantley (1998) of the FBI suggest that the logical step is for law enforcement agencies to go to the source, establishing direct contact and dialogue with militia groups. "Proactive contacts," as the two agents phrase them, should be made with militia leaders in order to defuse concerns and discuss issues in a nonconfrontational climate (1998, 2). Duffy and Brantley advocate a stance of greater openness, more effective communication, and more rational assessment and understanding of militias. By these efforts, they argue that anxiety on the part of militia members may be reduced and that crisis situations will have a greater chance of being resolved without violence. Likewise, the researcher Mack Marani has noted in his concluding assessments of the Michigan Militia ". . . that in some cases (Marani's emphasis) the effort to stigmatize militia members may come at a price" ("The Michigan Militia: Political Engagement or Political Alienation," *Terrorism and Political Violence* (Winter 1998), 10 (4): 141).

Preestablished contacts by local law enforcement officers have proven to be of significant value. Duffy and Brantley cite a barricade situation in Louisiana as an instance where the prior contacts between law enforcement officials and militia leaders enabled authorities to dispel rumors in their discussion with militia and resulted, ultimately, in the peaceful surrender of the militia suspect (1998, 3). A policy of open communications with militia leaders must, of course, be tempered by the realistic conclusion that some militia groups and/or members are not going to be open to dialogue due to their previously established views of the government and its agents, as well as their chosen set of tactics in confrontational situations.[4]

Effective responses toward terrorism as seen by effective efforts combating terrorism here and abroad put a high priority on personal, individual detection, infiltration, undermining, and arrest of terrorist perpetrators and groups. This type of police activity is practiced by the states and by federal authorities in the war on drugs in America. Though this kind of policing stands as a possible model for combating terrorism, it has not been prevalent. The 1993 bombing of the World Trade Center in New York was responded to *post hoc,* with little known about the Islamic group responsible for the action until information was put together piecemeal after the bombing. Indeed, much of what built the prosecution's case against the conspirators was the evidence and testimony provided by one of the conspirators himself. The infamous "Unabomber" case was broken after years of law enforcement frustration mostly because of information voluntarily provided by Ted Kaczynski's brother. Even Timothy McVeigh was initially apprehended, in a sense, due to luck of circumstances as he was found driving without a license plate on an interstate highway north of Oklahoma City.

Anti-Terrorism Methods of Other Countries

Time and again the success of law enforcement efforts against terrorists has been the result of chance, or perhaps fate, rather than of effective investigation and infiltration. Perhaps our national terrorism-related policies could be made more effective through an examination and application of ideas and methods from other countries that have had success in thwarting their domestic terrorists. The example of the Italian authorities' response to the Red Army of the 1970s is instructive here. According to author Cindy Combs (1997, 192), a combination of legal efforts and aggressive law enforcement led to a significant drop in terrorist attacks after 1980. Almost 2,000 suspected terrorists were imprisoned; most were members of the Brigades. Politically, laws were changed to enable police to detain suspects longer, to conduct warrantless searches, and to free authorities to use more wiretaps, surveillance, and detention/interrogation to combat terrorists. Further, in 1982 Italy passed a law which promised "repentant" terrorists lighter sentences if they confessed, resulting in a larger number of confession among Brigade members than ever before. Patrizio Peci, a former Brigade commander from Turin, was among the *pentiti* (repentant) (Combs 1997, 192). This substantial political and legal effort was directed by Interior Minister Virginio Rogoni and police general Carlo Della Chiesa, who were appointed in the wake of the kidnaping/murder of former Prime Minister Aldo Moro by the Red Brigades. The Italian Red Brigades were, as Laqueur recounts, defeated through a concerted campaign in which the authorities relied upon reductions in sentence in order to secure confessions and information (Laqueur 1987, 131). The *pentiti* provided important information about prior Brigade actions (e.g., the Aldo Moro kidnaping and murder) and cell supplies, resources and international networking (Laqueur 1987, 131). Internal dissent also played a role in the demise of the Red Brigades (Laqueur 1987, 132).

Other groups, such as the Uruguayan Tupamaros, also fell to similar tactics. A major leadership defection resulted in significant discoveries and arrests by the police. However, as Hacker (1976, 57) points out, the Uruguayan military's involvement in that country's counterterrorism effort resulted in part in the overthrow of the government and the establishment of a military dictatorship. Also the Basque separatist ETA, a notoriously ruthless and tight-knit group of northern Spain, has even had more than its share of terrorists who later cooperated with the police (Hacker 1976, 132).

The lessons to be learned from the Italian and Uruguayan successes are several. First, to combat terrorists, the equivalent of a "full court press" of political, legal and law enforcement measures must be undertaken. Second, this pressure may require an increase in the flexibility of police investigative and interrogative techniques and requires the nation's political representatives, citizens and judges to face and resolve some fundamental, difficult choices regarding the array of rights of due process for terrorist suspects. Third, the government must be willing to operate with a useful measure of reciprocity with those who are informants, defectors, or repentants from terrorist groups. The Italians would not have had the level of success in stifling the Red Brigades if not for the new laws which allowed for a reduction in sentence for the repentants. Though bargaining, leniency, commutations of sentence, and lobbying on behalf of a defendant turned witness is hardly uncommon in "ordinary" criminal cases, the government tends to avoid use of such negotiating tactics in terrorist cases. As Stephen Bowman points out in his work *When the Eagle Screams* and as the U.S. Department of State points out in its report, "Patterns of Global Terrorism," the counterterrorist policy of the U.S. stresses first and foremost that Americans can ". . . make no deals with terrorists and do not submit to blackmail" *U.S. Department of State* (1996, 1). Apparently, "no deals" means, in practice, no deals either before or after apprehension. Terrorists are not to be coddled and not to be bargained with, resulting in a loss of valuable information about and greater accessability to the terrorist enclaves from which they sprang.

Consultants Advocate Anti-Terrorism Measures

Perhaps lessons may also be learned from the advice and analysis of such consultants and writers on terrorism as Francis Watson (1976). Watson argues effectively that institutional efforts to combat terrorism must be made at the point at which terrorist cells are being formed (1976, 219). The cycle of terrorist activity and violence begins in terrorist group formation, as some people coalesce to attack the avowed evils of the age through violence. Though general in his recommendations, Watson does accentuate the need for public and private institutions in an aggrieved society to examine, clarify, promote, and live up to the core social and political values which serve as the foundation for the national system. In this effort at value clarification and enhancement, the government and important social and economic institutions must be honest, Watson argues (1976, 219), and not push real instances of injustice and corruption under the rug. Following Watson's suggestions, society facing a terrorist threat would, as a first order of business, openly and thoroughly discuss the critical national issues and try to come to a conclusion about where, as a nation, it stands.

According to Watson, trying to attack terrorists full-bore at the phase of propaganda and recruitment which follows initial organization, while producing results, creates risks to traditional civil liberties, such as freedom of the press and speech (1976, 219). Furthermore, to emphasize only intelligence and police activities in response to terrorists' strategies and violent actions will be to constantly place the political institutions in a reactionary posture, playing catch-up to the next set of plans and operations of the terrorist groups (1976, 204). The difficulties to be seen in concentrating on propaganda and recruitment or intelligence and police action illustrate the fundamental problem of national system response to terrorism—it is relatively easy, in a free society or even in a semi-free society, to put the government and the other important institutions on the defensive. It seems easier to attack than to defend political and social values. In order to avoid the suppression of civil liberties for the majority of citizens and to, at the same time, establish fair and reasonable domestic security, it is necessary to approach the problem of terrorism in a thorough, detailed way, addressing it on all fronts. This is an extremely challenging but critical task. To avoid becoming the "garrison state" (borrowed from Cameron Hall's phrase regarding the McCarthy Red Scare of the Cold War, 1954) and at the same time prevent rampant lawlessness and social disintegration will not be easy to do.

America Needs Anti-Terrorism Debate

We hope that we have shown by the previous discussion that to truly be effective in responding to terrorism, America needs a debate about the real methods, tactics, and goals which it hopes to pursue in its assault on terrorists. Such a debate must also dispassionately analyze and assess the concerns of militia groups and extremists. The country needs to thoughtfully and deliberately consider the options open to it—politically, legally, constitutionally, and morally.

Interestingly, the framework for the kind of debate which is needed has been outlined, not by an American political leader, but by the former Prime Minister of Israel in his 1995 book *Fighting Terrorism: How Democracies Can Defeat Domestic and International Terrorists.* Benjamin Netanyahu has considerable experience in the field of counterterrorism as a diplomat, policy maker, researcher and writer on national security issues. Berl Faulbaum (1995), a media consultant and Internet book reviewer, has well indicated how the Israeli leader has described the history of world terrorism and has argued that the West has not adequately prepared itself for the increase in international and domestic terrorism. On the domestic front, Netanyahu (1995) advocates giving law enforcement authorities more power, while maintaining civil liberties through judicial and legislative overviews. Faulbaum (1995, 2) rightly indicates that the historic concerns for civil liberties in the United States prevents citizens or politicians from embracing Netanyahu's recommendations.

The Israeli political figure challenges western democracies to "wake up" and develop a clearer, more decisive response to terrorism. Netanyahu asserts that terrorism at home is serious and on the increase in terms of lethality and destructiveness, if not numbers. The United States needs to not play the world's Rip Van Winkle of terrorism. Leaders of the public and private sectors need to begin to lead the debate to frame appropriate social and political responses, including policy responses to the terrorist threat.

The "war" on terrorism will likely be won or lost, not by virtue of high-powered weaponry or massive manpower or by huge allotments of public revenue. Success or failure will come as a result of the organization, purpose, skill and intelligence of those involved in counterterrorism. As a first order of business, the agencies of the federal government, in a coordinated manner, need to establish as a priority the collection, analysis, and networking of vital information regarding the nature, resources, objectives and tactics of domestic terrorists and potential terrorist groups. Secondly, some agency, or perhaps, interagency task force with substantial legal authority and financial and logistical resources should be designated as the operational coordinating group on domestic terror, as the National Security Council is for international-based incidents.

Today, a possible pattern for such an organization to follow in the initial phase of policy direction is that of Interpol, the international crime fighting organization headquartered in France. In response to the dramatic spate of skyjackings in the 1960s, Interpol reassessed its longstanding prohibition against involvement in political crimes and fashioned a rational, flexible response to the problems at hand. The organization prepared a study of the skyjacking problem that served as instructive to all nations regarding preventive and punitive measures (Fooner 1973, 29). The report was then distributed to key international transportation and other pertinent agencies, the International Civil Aviation Organization, the United Nations General Assembly, and the International Air Transport Association. After much discussion at its general meetings of 1969 and 1970, Interpol decided in 1972 to use its facilities to help combat such forms of international crime as hijacking and terrorism. Skyjacking was to be treated like a common criminal offense for Interpol, as was the sending of letter bombs. Special multinational conferences convened by countries affected by airline terrorism helped to put pressure on Interpol to adopt policies of greater flexibility (Fooner 1973, 30). Furthermore, Interpol's General Assembly adopted a resolution in 1984 that states, "In general, offences are not considered to be political when they are committed outside a 'conflict area' and when the victims are not connected with the aims or objectives pursued by the offenders" ("Basic Principles of Interpol," *Interpol Web Page* 13 March 1998).

National Conference Also Important

Given the evolution of Interpol approaches to terrorism outlined by Michael Fooner, perhaps it is appropriate to suggest that, in order to build a more effective information network and analysis for domestic terrorism, the White House and the National Governor's Conference should, as soon as possible, convene a conference of the fifty states and the important federal law enforcement bodies to specifically discuss terrorist threats, terrorist potentiality, and suggestions for improvements in federal, state and intergovernmental policies toward domestic terrorism. As suggested also by Riley and Hoffman (1995, 4) such a national conference would also bring together law enforcement officials from all fields and geographic areas of the country in order to exchange information and build cooperation. The conference might well provide a basis for further effective lobbying of Congress and state legislatures for the strengthening of policies toward terrorists, similar to the effect multinational conferences on sky-terror had on Interpol in the early 1970s.

Further, since Interpol's constitution and eventual United Nations recognition supported its status as an intergovernmental organization working with other intergovernmental or nongovernmental organizations, Interpol was able to cross bureaucratic boundaries and establish effective working relationships with groups such as the Customs Cooperation Council, the European Committee on Crime Problems, the U.N. Commission on Narcotic Drugs and the Economic and Social Council (Fooner 1973, 74). Though largely untested, cross-agency cooperation at the federal level is possible in a domestic crisis in a most dramatic but untraditional fashion. While the Posse Comitatus Act prevents the armed forces from acting in a civil police capacity, presidents have the authority to waive these prohibitions if it is necessary to handle a specific incident. The FBI has prepared memoranda of understanding with the military in order to set out guidelines for any future joint operations of a counter-terrorist kind (Monroe 1982, 144).

Innovative Methods Have Been Devised

Innovative applications of criminal laws are also possible in the war against terrorists. The FBI's successful efforts in apprehending and convicting Croation terrorists bombers on the East Coast in 1980-81 was due to in part to application of the Racketeering-Influenced and Corrupt Organizations statute (RICO). RICO provides for long prison terms—20 years—$25,000 in fines, and the forfeiture of the fruits of any criminal enterprise. Croation terrorists were sentenced to between 20 and 35 years (Monroe 1982,

140). More recently, the National Commission on Terrorism established by Congress in 1998 recommended specifically that bureaucratic regulations now requiring CIA headquarters to approve recruitment of informants in the field who have had serious criminal infractions be removed. Agents in the field need more discretion in the use of informants, to follow the Commission's logic. The FBI was also urged to eliminate red tape when deciding whether to open a preliminary terrorist investigation (*Minneapolis Star Tribune* 4 June 2000, A4).

Another policy/law enforcement development we will surely see more of in the future is the creation and use of "smart," non-lethal weapons for counterterrorism, riot control, and response to hostage-takings and kidnapings. As the Tofflers have reported in their work *War and Anti-War* (1993), military and private researchers have been at work on a variety of nonlethal weapons. The Pentagon, the Global Strategy Council, and individual experts such as Janet and Chris Morris have researched and/or developed smart weapons. For example, infrasound generators, useful for crowd control and tested in France, are known to emit such low-frequency sound waves that those focused upon become disoriented and experience nausea and loss of bowel control (Toffler and Toffler 1993, 129). Weapons such as those of a sound or acoustic nature would seem to be well worthwhile as compared to traditional military or law enforcement weapons and the carnage they frequently leave behind. William J. Taylor, Jr. of the Center for Strategic and International Studies in Washington, D.C., cites as examples the Bosnian and Somalian conflicts and the Waco, TX, incident here at home to illustrate problems with the use of lethal weaponry in low-intensity situations and the need for nonlethal alternatives (Toffler and Toffler 1993, 130). Nonlethal weapons will surely be in high demand in terror-response and terror-prevention operations by governmental and nongovernmental institutions in the future.

Interpol Is Underfunded

In recent years, the major developed nations (the P-8, formerly known as G-7[5]), especially the United States, have pushed for tougher international approaches to extradition, money laundering, drug trafficking, official corruption, financial/technological crime, and asset seizure against known terrorists (Malinowski 1998, 2). Evidence of this resurgent effort to achieve greater international cooperation in the fight against terrorists and other criminals may be seen in the proposed International Crime Control Act unveiled by the Clinton administration on May 12, 1998 (*Tulsa World,* 13 May 1998, A-6). The proposal is intended to stimulate efforts to prevent and prosecute terrorists and other criminals. Tracking, capturing, and expeditiously extraditing offenders who cross national borders are seen as the proper international objectives of this new approach. Special attention from the proposal is directed toward drug traffickers, counterfeiters, and those engaged in industrial espionage. Though the bill has its congressional critics, namely Senator Pat Coverdell (R-GA), head of a Senate Foreign Relations Panel on Drugs and Terrorism, it serves as a major agenda item for P-8 economic summit meetings such as the one in Birmingham, England, in May 1998 (*Tulsa World* 13 May 1998, A-6). However, leaders at Interpol have bemoaned the fact that, amid all of this political and legal jousting of "getting tough on terrorists," as the only law enforcement organization that spans the globe, Interpol is provided only $30 million annually to operate by member governments, including the U.S. This sum has often not been increased in successive years (Malinowski 1998, 2). Therefore, when looking at the future, one may question just what role member governments want Interpol to play in fighting terrorist crimes.

U.S. Funding Also Meager

Interpol's funding struggle parallels the funding shortfalls which are evidence in U.S. national appropriations devoted to combating terrorism abroad and, most significantly, at home. The single phrase which stands out in descriptions of the funding for counterterrorism efforts is "ad hoc budgeting," and it is found in the General Accounting Office (GAO) Report to Congressional Requesters on December 1, 1997. From the GAO Report to Representative Ike Skelton (D - Missouri) and Senator John Glenn (D-Ohio), the following quote stands as a near indictment of the haphazard, scattershot nature of terrorism-related funding:

> The amount of federal funds being spent on programs and activities to combat terrorism is unknown and difficult to determine. Identifying and tracking terrorism-related government-wide spending with precision is difficult for several reasons, such as the lack of a uniform definition of terrorism

and the inclusion of these expenditures within larger categories that do not really allow separation (1997, 3).

Indeed, as the GAO (1997, 4) indicated, terrorism-related spending is uncertain (4). While the GAO found a total of nearly $7 bil-
lion spent on unclassified federal efforts related to terrorism for
fiscal year 1997, complete data for the two departments which
spend the largest share of estimated funds, currently Defense
(DOD) and Energy, could not be found for 1994 or 1995 (*GAO*
Table 1.1 December 1997, 6). DOD and Energy make up 54.8 and
21.2%, respectively, of the total estimated unclassified spending
on terrorism issues (*GAO* Figure 1.1 December 1997, 7). Problems,
including a lack of priorities and basic inadequacy, abound. Note
this passage from the GAO report:

> There is no interagency mechanism to centrally manage fund-
> ing requirements and requests to ensure an efficient, focused
> government-wide application of federal funds to numerous
> agencies' programs designed to combat terrorism (1997, 7).

Under the Presidential Decision Directive (PDD) 39, listed earlier in this chapter in the policy chronology, the National Security
Council is to coordinate policy issues while the OMB is to assess
alternative funding demands related to terrorism spending. However,
neither agency is required to collect, aggregate, and review funding
and spending as they relate to terrorism. Analysis across departments, with an eye toward building a comprehensive governmental
strategy on counterterrorism, is sorely messy. Validation of risk and
threat and priority in spending is, according to the GAO (1997, 3)
very inadequate. Throughout the GAO report of December 1997, the
lack of sufficient analysis, data, and comparison to make intelligent, strategic choices about funding challenges in response to terrorism are mentioned. Basically, then, despite some legislative and
executive effort in the aftermath of the Oklahoma City bombing, the
federal government has a reactionary approach to policy related to
terrorism at best, as we have contended earlier in this chapter (See
Figures 4.1 and 4.2 [page 113 and 117].)

We Need a Plan

Given the facts and circumstances surrounding terrorism-related
policymaking as we have described above, it is no wonder that the
response of the government to domestic terrorist incidents seems

often confusing, ineffective and uncoordinated. Priority-setting, strategy development, interdepartmental and intergovernmental analysis, management, planning and evaluation are either absent in policy formation and administration or applied in a disjointed, erratic manner. As terrorism scholar Robert Kupperman pointed out almost 15 years ago in a work provided for the National Commission on Violence, a society facing a terrorist threat should react on three hierarchical levels. The terrorist incident should first be isolated and contained. Second, effective "damage control" must take place so as to deal with political and other consequences of the incident on the domestic or international front. Third, the government must use the incident after the fact as a means of honing and improving national policy in response to terrorism (in Curtis 1985, 199-200). As our previous discussions of domestic terrorist-style incidents and federal policy development toward terrorism indicate, the U.S. government has not often followed Kupperman's policy framework very effectively. Historians, like philosophers, often express the view of human behavior that we cannot know where we are truly headed in the future if we do not learn about and know where we have been.

If the emphasis on knowing the past in order to make better decisions in the future may be applied to counterterrorism policy-making against domestic threats, it may be fairly said that our governmental response to terrorism reflects that we have not adequately understood where we've been; also, we do not have a very clear picture of where we are, given the GAO Report of December 1997 and the lack of uniform data and analysis of counterterrorism funding. Because of the uncertainties surrounding the past and present of terrorist-related policies, we have not seemed to know where we are going with counterterrorism policy.

One possible "roadmap" has recently been put forward, however, by the final phase of the report of the U.S. Commission on National Security/21st Century (a separate group from the Commission on Terrorism mentioned earlier in this chapter) of January 31, 2001. Phase III of the Commission Report, entitled *Road Map for National Security: Imperative for Change* (www.nssg.gov) offers recommendations in five major areas of policy: 1) *ensuring* security in the American homeland; 2) *racapitalizing* on U.S. strengths in science and education; 3) *redesigning* institutional structure and response in the executive branch of government; 4) *overhauling* the U.S. personnel system; and 5) reorganizing Congress's role in national security (from the "Executive Summary," viii). The Commission, chaired by former Senators Warren Rudman and Gary Hart, was comprised of recognized national security experts and former cabinet-level officials. One of the most significant recommendations made by the Commission was a call for the creation of an independent National Homeland Security Agency (NHSA) with responsibility for organizing all services of U.S. government activity involved in homeland security ("Executive Summary," viii). The proposals put forward by the Commission are a dramatic recognition of the need to change counter-terrorism strategy and policy for this country. The ideas should be given diligent consideration by Congress and the White House in fashioning comprehensive national security policy. The danger is that the recommendations now made public will be lost in the normal maze of interest group politics that has come to dominate the federal agenda.[6]

Notes

1. As Busby indicated to the Senate Permanent Subcommittee on Investigations, the 4 Pillars of official counterterrorism policy established in 1986 are: 1) Intelligence collection and analysis; 2) Law enforcement and prosecution; 3) Diplomacy and coordination; 4) Operations and training.

2. See Cobb and Elder (1972) for a discussion of policy agendas which stem from triggering events.

3. See Braybrooke and Lindbloom (1963) for a thorough critique and explanation of incrementalist policymaking.

4. For example, the militant group The Order as described by Baradat (1997, 285) and most recently the Four Corners Survivalists, Pilon, McVean and Mason who caused a massive manhunt in Utah, Colorado, New Mexico and Arizona in the summer of 1998.

5. The P-8 includes Britain, Canada, France, Germany, Italy, Japan, Russia and the U.S.

6. Unfortunately, the recommendations of the Hart/Rudman Commission received minimal consideration in Washington, D.C., until the catastrophic terrorist attacks of September 11, 2001, on New York City and the Pentagon. A part of President George W. Bush's domestic response to those attacks has been to create a cabinet-level Office of Homeland Security, with former governor Tom Ridge of Pennsylvania as the director.

Chapter Discussion Questions

1. Describe and explain the purpose and content of PDD 39, established by President Clinton in the aftermath of the Oklahoma City bombing in 1995.

2. Identify and describe, in general, the basic elements of the Reactionary-Incrementalist Model of Counterterrorism Policy. Illustrate and develop your own model for describing counterterrorism policy.

3. What happened to the alleged political extremists and to law enforcement officials during the incident at Ruby Ridge, ID? How does this incident illustrate the Reactionary-Incrementalist Model of Counterterrorism Policy?

4. Discuss the problems of a) lack of coordination and b) haphazard funding in relation to Federal agencies and counterterrorism policy.

5. What role do the states play in current policies related to terrorism and why?

6. Briefly discuss the Antiterrorism and Effective Death Penalty Act of 1996.

7. Define:

   a. Incremental

   b. Reactive

   c. Federalism

8. Overall, what lessons may be learned form the experiences of other countries or of international organizations in fighting terrorism.

Suggestions for Further Reading

Duffey and Brantly. "Militia: Initiating Contact," Internet/FBI Academy. 2 May 1009.

Lois Ember. 1996. "FBI Takes the Lead in Developing Counterterrorism Effort." *Chemical and Engineering News.* 4 November.

FBI—The Basics. "The Basics of Terrorism—Part 1-6," Internet/ Terrorism Research Center. 1997-1998.

Brent L. Smith. 1994. *Terrorism in America: Pipe Bombs and Pipe Dreams.* Albany: State University of New York Press.

U.S. GAO. "Report to Congressional Requesters—Combating Terrorism," Internet/Terrorism Research Center. 5 December 1997.

J. Brent Wilson. 1994. "The United States' Response to International Terrorism," In *The Deadly Sin of Terrorism.* Ed. David A. Charters. Westport, CT: Greenwood Press.

CHAPTER VI

Conclusion

"Crime can never be controlled through the criminal justice system alone. Even the most powerful and arbitrary police state in a simple rural environment will be unable to frustrate the deep desires and secret acts of people."

—Ramsey Clark. 1971.
Crime in America. New York: Pocket, 99.

Response to the domestic terrorist threat requires, more than anything, a change in the cultural mind-set of Americans. We must accept the possibility, indeed the probability, that "we" (in our many institutional, organizational and cultural aspects) are vulnerable. Strategically, we have often used *realpolitik* in our determined pursuit of national interest abroad, yet behaved naïvely and ignorantly when it came to preparing for the possible disastrous behavior of our own citizens. We can afford this ostrich-like position in relation to domestic terrorist issues no more.

Indeed, the school shootings at Columbine High in Littleton, CO, in April of 1999 served to dislodge the ostrich of American society from its comfort zone of ignoring violence, if only for the short term. Professing an admiration of Hitler and the dress and values of the so-called Goth culture, students Harris and Klebold stormed their own high school with lethal force on April 20 (Hitler's birthday) and killed 12 fellow students and one teacher before turning their weapons on themselves, each ending his own life (Andrew Phillips, "Lessons of Littleton," *Maclean's,* 3 May 1999, 18-21). The Goth lifestyle that seemed such a basis for the attitudes and dress of the "Trenchcoat Mafia," to which Harris and Klebold belonged at Columbine High, has its contemporary roots in the post-punk rock band following in Great Britain. Black dress; painted white faces contrasting with dark makeup; preoccupation with death in speech and writing; obsession with fantasy computer games such as *Dungeons and Dragons;* these aspects of Goth culture seem to have become prominent in the way American teenagers have often incorporated Goth values into their own social environment (Damian Whitworth, "Gloomy tribal craze that was born in Britain," *The Times* [London], 22 April 1999, 5).

While the shootings in Colorado served notice with some finality that violence in American society can and will threaten any social institution, much of the public and political discussion afterward focused on the instruments of death—the weapons—and the demand for greater regulation or limitation of access to guns. What remains for the most part missing in the discussion of violence, it seems, is a greater recognition of the need to study and evaluate more realistically the "warning signs" of such destructive behavior and to study such signs more rigorously and systematically.

The need for greater awareness, attention and study on the part of all members of the social community was brought home to author Rodgers in the course of an interview with a knowledgeable and active middle-aged male citizen of a major southeastern Idaho community of about 50,000 people. This individual has served on his city's drug and gang education community board that is comprised of citizens, educators, and health and law enforcement officials. "Our community is extremely naïve," indicated this individual in describing the problems of gangs, violence, and hate in the city's schools. "Professional conferences for awareness education do exist and teachers, especially, should attend, but follow-through with more teachers, parents, and community groups is needed" (personal interview, 6 May 1999). Learning is not always effectively shared, in other words.

There is a definite need for follow-through for better coordination of efforts between groups and institutions trying to address hate crime violence in our communities. In recounting an instance of anti-Semitic hate graffiti sprayed on three business buildings in a southeastern Idaho community, one police officer (a veteran of more than 20 years experience and a leader in community-services policing relating to race/hate issues) related to Rodgers that the incident was reported to the local human rights committee of the community, but no response or review of the matter ever came out (phone interview, 10 May 1999). In absence of an identifiable suspect (who often never emerges), law enforcement officials are frequently limited in what they can do. Political/social groups that are ostensibly charged with the responsibility for investigating, reviewing and speaking out about such incidents might want to take greater advantage of their symbolic power and issue prompt statements, not only to serve notice that the community is watching and is vigilant, but also that any act of public intolerance is a cause for concern. *Don't despair of raising awareness and taking a stand* might be a healthy guideline for human rights committees to follow.

Coordination among institutional actors in the battle against hate, intolerance and the violence that accompanies them is crucial. According to an experienced law enforcement officer of 16 years who is knowledgeable about violent hate crimes in both Idaho and California and is currently involved in the Gang Task Force for Southeast Idaho, a significant thing that hinders coordination is the absence of a uniform national hate crimes data base. Communication and coordination across jurisdictions, across state lines, and across levels of government authority are keys to greater success in deterring and responding to violence. Problems occur because officials at different levels use different definitions. What a gang is, for instance, may be defined differently depending on locale. There is a need to get beyond disputes over definitions, to do what is effective, and to look at the desired outcomes in terms of policing and social effects. Strategy, communication and coordination must be fashioned to fit the outcomes a society/community wants (personal interview, 12 May 1999).

To illustrate the current difficulty in responding to violence in community and nation, let's consider the problems of strategy development and implementation concerning the recent high-profile issue of random school violence. Looking at all of the recommendations concerning school violence mentioned in the aftermath of shootings such as those that occurred in Littleton, CO, in April 1999 or in Ft. Gibson, OK, in December of the same year, the authors are struck by how passive and/or reactive they are.

Typically, proposals have concentrated on improving security and detection measures at schools, mostly at the point at which students are to enter the main building. Some proposals (e.g., workshops on violence) also advocate improved education and awareness programs for teachers and students. Still others concentrate on improving procedures for responding to an incident of violence once it occurs. On the whole, proposals are notable for their *lack* of proactive, socially-directed manner and perspective.

In typical American public policymaking fashion we search for a solution to a significant problem in the "symptoms" of the problem rather than its root causes, which are much harder to discern (see Cyert and March, *Behavioral Theory of the Firm,* 1963). Having seen the symptoms, we frequently embrace the first, most feasible alternative or set of alternatives that arise from our deliberations—somewhat akin to taking the teaspoonful of cough syrup which will suppress our hacking for a few hours without treating the underlying condition behind the cough. In Herbert Simon's view (1976) we "satisfice" in our decision, not having the time or resources to do more, or not being willing to devote more time and resources to the problem. Sometimes, it would appear that the social authorities and the significant people connected to those who commit terroristic violence don't even so much as "satisfice," but rather look the other way when tension builds until an unfortunate tragedy occurs as in the Columbine shooting previously recounted. (See for instance *WKBT-Channel 8* News at 10, "Covering Our World" [segment] 17, May 2001 report of a commission report in Colorado critical of local law enforcement authorities in Littleton, CO, for ignoring warning statements and signs given by perpetrators in months leading up to the school massacre.)

Most proposals that have come forward in response to the many violent incidents—acts of terrorism—discussed in this book are of the "satisficing" variety. They tackle symptoms. One persistent set of suggestions is directed at possible sources of violence and is intended to regulate or change general social behavior contributing to violence: the ideas that have been put forward advocating stricter gun control measures. However, these proposed regulations typically create determined opposition in the political arena, as they fly in the face of the traditional American view of the virtues of individual control over weapons and the committed constitutional views of a powerful lobby, the National Rifle Association. The political environment being what it is, the idea of further significant gun control is hardly likely to pass the Congress and be signed by the President in time to have a serious impact on the problem of spasmodic, terroristic violence.

While foolproof solutions to spasmodic violence will no doubt elude us, we can use better strategies for dealing with the problem than we have to date. Often, national emergencies or crises of faith provide the spark for the creation of more proactive and extensive proposals for combating social ills (e.g., the Depression and FDR's New Deal; persistent poverty and race discrimination and LBJ's Great Society; tax protest movements and low confidence in the federal government and the Reagan Revolution). Each of the crises and corresponding government responses hinged upon the development of an effective political coalition, mobilized in the wake of the social problem(s), to build and sustain the political solutions.

Spasmodic violence is a *major* social problem in search of an effective coalition. Until churches, schools and governments (particularly at the local level) *combine* efforts to develop strategies and programs to *prevent* violence, we will see the periodic bombings, shootings and maimings continue in a senseless haze of national confusion . Wheeler and Baron's *Violence in Our Schools, Hospitals and Public Places* (1994) is one resource that could assist civic groups in their development of an overall plan to prevent and respond to acts of terrorism and terroristic violence. The book is rich in analysis of the problems of violence and provides many suggestions for plans and security measures to prevent violence in public places.

Community outreach programs need to be established, enlisting the efforts of counselors, law enforcement personnel, pastors, and teachers, to work at identifying and evaluating at-risk situations in communities and to promote through all available media assistance that can be accessed by families and schools so they can identify at-risk children and promote nonviolent conflict resolution at home, at school, and at work. In short, the problem of spasmodic violence will not be addressed very successfully until— somewhat like clean air and water protection in the 1970s—it is seen as everyone's issue and everyone's responsibility. As a foundation, the major social institutions (education, family, politics, and religion) must seriously focus on the issue and be willing to join together to do something comprehensive about it. Clarity, coordination and purpose—striving for prevention as well as better reaction to terrorism at home in America—comprise perhaps the trio of goals government agencies (from the federal level on down) can begin to emphasize with greater public relations zeal and more resources.

Chapter Discussion Questions

1. What are some of the problems which currently make governmental responses to terrorism and terroristic violence very haphazard and difficult to accomplish?

2. In your own words, suggest some ways that local communities might better address the threats of terrorism and terroristic violence.

Suggestions for Further Reading

Phillips, Andrew. 1999. "Lessons of Littleton." *Maclean's*. 3 May.

Simon, Herbert. 1976. *Administrative Behavior,* 3rd edition. New York: Macmillan.

Wheeler, Eugene D. and S. Anthony Baron. 1994. *Violence in our Schools, Hospitals and Public Places: A Prevention and Management Guide.* Ventura, CA: Pathfinder Publishing.

Whitworth, Damian. 1999. "Gloomy tribal craze that was born in Britain." *The Times* [London]. 22 April.

Epilogue

The purpose of this book has been to engage the reader in a meaningful dialogue concerning the nature and consequences of extremist politics and terrorism, specifically on the domestic front. As this text was being prepared for publication, the United States tragically experienced the most disastrous terrorist incidents in its history with the hijacked airliner crashes that destroyed the twin towers of the World Trade Center in New York City, damaged the Pentagon in Washington D.C., and plowed into the unpopulated countryside of Somerset County, PA. September 11, 2001 brought home to America an almost overwhelming fear and loss as thousands of citizens were either killed, injured or unaccounted for in the wake of the terrorist attacks.

While our focus has been on the domestic sources of terror in America, we recognize once again that our homeland is indeed vulnerable, as we have tried to point out, from terrorist acts from multiple sources, especially those directed at what are traditionally considered civilian targets. We are convinced of the need for continued dialogue and study into the scourge of terrorism and will commit our own energies to continued investigation and research into the circumstances surrounding the attack on American soil in September, 2001.

Terms to Know

Students and other readers will benefit by developing brief descriptions for each of the following items in order to fashion a more complete understanding of key concepts. Information provided in the text provides the basis for useful descriptions for each item; however, in a few cases (e.g., international issues), supplemental research may provide for enhanced learning about the subjects listed here.

ACLU—American Civil Liberties Union

American Renaissance

Anarchism

ANO—Abu Nidal Organization

Antichrist

1996 Anti-terrorism Act

Arizona Patriots

Army of God

Article I, Section 8, paragraph 16, U.S. Constitution

Aryan Nations

Branch Davidians

British Israelism

CSA—Covenant Sword and Arm of the Lord

Christian Constitutionalists

Christian Patriots

Church of the Creator

Church of Jesus Christ Christian (Aryan Nations)

Elohim City, OK

Federalism

FEMA—Federal Emergency Management Agency

References

Abcarian, Gilbert and Sherman M. Stange. 1965. "Alienation and the Radical Right." *Journal of Politics* 27:776-796.

Academy for Counterterrorism Education. 1998. Internet/New Mexico Tech and Louisiana State Universities. 22 May.

ALPHA.org [links to other organizations]. 1998. 14 August.

Aho, James A. 1990. *The Politics of Righteousness: Idaho Christian Patriotism.* Seattle: University of Washington Press.

———. 1994. *This Thing of Darkness: A Sociology of the Enemy.* Seattle: University of Washington Press.

Armond, Paul de. 1997. "Putting the Far Right into Perspective." *Public Good Project, Internet* (Accessed 1 June 1999).

Ashby, LeRoy and Rod Gramer. 1994. *Fighting the Odds: The Life of Senator Frank Church.* Pullman, WA: Washington State University Press.

Baradat, Leon P. 1997. *Political Ideologies: Their Origins and Impact,* 6th ed. Upper Saddle River, NJ: Prentice Hall.

Barkun, Michael. Editor. 1996. *Millennialism and Violence.* Portland, OR: Frank Cass.

Beam, L.R. 1998. "The Conspiracy to Erect an Electronic Iron Curtain." *Stormfront, Internet,* 21 July.

Bennett, David H. 1995. *The Party of Fear: The American Far Right from Nativism to the Militia Movement,* revised and updated. New York: Vintage Books.

"Bo Gritz says FBI has enlisted him in Rudolph search." 1998. *CNN, interactive* [CNN.com], 3 August.

Bowman, Stephen. 1994. *When the Eagle Screams: America's Vulnerability to Terrorism.* New York: Birch Lane Press.

Braybrooke, David and Charles E. Lindbloom. 1963. *A Strategy of Decision: Policy Evaluation as a Social Process.* New York: Free Press.

Bushart, Howard L. and John R. Craig and Myra Barnes. 1998. *Soldiers of God: White Supremacists and Their Holy War for America.* New York: Kensington Books.

Canadian Department of Justice. 1998. *Disproportionate Harm: Hate crime in Canada* (Tables 1-9; Conclusion) [Internet]. 15 August.

Cash, J. D. 1998. "Bombshell!!! The Rev. Robert Millar Identified as FBI Informant." *McCurtain Daily Gazette* (July 1997). [www.Free Republic.com] 30 July.

CBS Evening News. 1997. 24 March.

CBS, 48 Hours. 1997. 17 July.

CBS Reports. 1997. 25 March .

Chenoweth, Helen. 1998. "America in Crisis" (videotape). *Militia of Montana.* Noxon, MT, housed in General Curriculum Collections, Albertson's Library—Boise State University. Boise, ID.

Chenoweth for Congress, web site. www.helenchenoweth.org/.

Christian Constitutionalist. 1999. Phone conversation. 3 May. Boise, ID.

CNG [Cyber Nationalist Group, Internet]. 1998. "Suppressed Facts Page (II)," 14 August.

Coates, James. 1987. *Armed and Dangerous: The Rise of the Survivalist Right.* New York: Hill and Wang.

Cobb, Roger W. and Charles P. Elder. 1972. *Participation in American Politics: The Dynamics of Agenda-Building.* Boston: Allyn and Bacon.

Cohn, Norman. 1995. *Cosmos, Chaos and the World to Come: The Ancient Roots of Apocalyptic Faith.* New Haven, CT: Yale University Press.

Cohn, Norman. 1970. *The Pursuit of the Millennium,* revised and expanded edition. New York: Oxford University Press.

Cohn, Norman. 1967. *Warrant for Genocide: The Myth of the Jewish World Conspiracy and the Protocols of the Elders of Zion.* London: Oxford University Press.

Combs, Cindy C. 1997. *Terrorism in the Twenty-First Century.* Upper Saddle River, NJ: Prentice Hall.

Connolly, Ceci and Helen Dewar. 1998. "Duke Prepares Bid for Livingston's Seat" *Washington Post, Internet edition,* 18 February.

Cotler, Irwin. 1998. "Towards a counter-Terrorism Law and Policy." *Terrorism and Political Violence* 10(2):1-14.

Cyert, Richard M. and James March. 1963. *A Behavioral Theory of the Firm.* Englewood Cliffs, NJ: Prentice Hall.

Daily Oklahoman. 2000. [ad for Hall of Fame Gun and Knife Show]. 28 April.

Daily Oklahoman. 1995. May–June issues.

DCI News. 1998. "Militia/Patriot Movement." 29 July.

Dobson, Christopher and Ronald Payne. 1982. *The Terrorists: Their Weapons, Leaders and Tactics,* revised edition. New York: Facts on File, Inc.

Douglass, Joseph D., Jr. and Neil C. Livingstone. 1987. *America the Vulnerable.* Lexington, MA: Lexington Books.

Duffey, James E. and Alan C. Brantley. 1998. "Militias: Initiating Contact," Internet/FBI Academy, 22 May.

Dyer, Joel. 1997. *Harvest of Rage: Why Oklahoma City Is Only the Beginning.* Boulder, CO: Westview Press

Easton, David. 1971. *The Political System,* 2nd ed. New York: Alfred A. Knopf.

Ember, Lois. 1996. "FBI Takes the Lead in Developing Counterterrorism Effort." *Chemical and Engineering News,* 4 November.

English, Paul. 1995. "State Strugles to Find Money for Bomb Costs." *Daily Oklahoman.* 19 May.

Falwell, Jerry. 1981. *The Fundamentalist Phenomenon: The Resurgence of Conservative Christianity.* Garden City, NY: Doubleday-Galilee.

Faulbaum, Berl. 1995. "How Should This Nation Battle Terrorism?" Review of Benjamin Netanyahu's *Fighting Terrorism.* Internet/*Detroit News*–Bookshelf, 22 November.

Federal Bureau of Investigation. 1997-1998. "The Basics of Terrorism— Part 1-6." Internet/Terrorism Research Center. 1997-1998.

Ferkiss, Victor. 1954. "The Political and Economic Philosophy of American Fascism." Ph.D. dissertation. The University of Chicago.

Flynn, Kevin and Gary Gerhardt. 1989. *The Silent Brotherhood.* New York: The Free Press.

Fooner, Michael. 1973. *Interpol: The Inside Story of the International Crime Fighting Organization.* Chicago: Henry Regnery Co.

Frantzich, Stephen E. and Steven E. Schier. 1995. *Congress: Games and Strategies.* Madison, WI: Brown and Benchmark.

Fromm, Eric. 1964. *The Heart of Man: Its Genius for Good and Evil.* New York: Harper & Row.

Fuller, Robert. 1996. *Naming the Antichrist: The History of an American Obsession.* New York: Oxford University Press.

George, John and Laird Wilcox. 1996. *American Extremists: Militias, Supremacists, Klansmen, Communists, and Others.* New York: Prometheus Books.

Gallup Organization—Princeton, Internet. 1998. "Congress Job Approval," data from Apr. 1974–May 10, 1998. 15 August.

———. 1998. "Satisfaction With U.S.," data from Feb. 1979–May 10, 1998. 15 August.

———. 2000. "Congress Job Approval," data from March 1992–January 2000 [gallup.com/poll/trends/ptjobapp-Cong.asp] 19 May.

———. 2000. "Presidential Approval Ratings" April 28–30, 2000. 19 May.

Gillert, Douglas J. 1998. "Terrorism Expert Sounds Battle Cry." *Armed Forces Press Service,* 1 April.

Graff, James, Patrick E. Cole and Elaine Shannon. 1998. "The White City on a Hill." *Time, online,* 149(8), 24 February.

Hacker, Frederick J. 1976. *Crusaders, Criminals, Crazies: Terror and Terrorism in Our Time.* New York: W.W. Norton.

Hall, Cameron P. 1954. "McCarthyism—An Analysis," *Social Action,* Vol. 21, September.

Harris, John F. 1996. *Washington Post* [Internet–*Legi-Slate* article]. 25 April.

Hart, Gary. 1998. *The Minuteman: Restoring an Army of the People.* New York: Free Press.

Harvest-trust, Web pages. 1999. "Trojan Horse, etc." 1 April. 1–7.

Headline News. 1998. CNN. 2 February.

Hensley, Dennis E. 1998. *Millennium Approaches.* New York: Avon Books.

Higham, John. 1977. *Strangers in the Land: Patterns of American Nativism 1860–1925.* 2nd ed. New York: Atheneum.

Hinton, Carla. 1995. "Boy's Recovery Reflected in His Grin." Daily *Oklahoman.* 2 June.

Hoffer, Eric. 1951. *The True Believer.* New York: Harper and Row.

Hoffman, Bruce. 1999. "Terrorism Trends and Prospects" in *Countering the New Terrorism,* Ian O. Lesser et al. Santa Monica CA: RAND. 7-35.

Hofstadter, Richard. 1996. *The Paranoid Style in American Politics* (first paper edition). Cambridge, MA: Harvard University Press.

Holy Bible. King James Version.

"Israeli Chopper Crash." 1997. *Maclean's,* 17 February.

Jackman, Robert W. 1987. "Political Institutions and Voter Turnout in the Industrial Democracies." *American Political Science Review* 81: 420.

Johnston, Carla Brooks. 1998. "Radical Radio Redux." *Intelligence Report* [Southern Poverty Law Center] Summer (91).

Jones, Stephen and Peter Israel. 1998. *Others Unknown: The Oklahoma City Bombing Case and Conspiracy.* New York: Public Affairs.

Junas, Daniel. 1995. "Rise of Citizen Militias: Angry White Guys with Guns." *Covert Action Quarterly* Spring (52).

Keating, Hon. Frank. 1996. *Speaking Frankly Homepage* (Oklahoma Governor's Office). April.

Koenig, Louis W. 1996. *The Chief Executive,* 6th ed. Fort Worth: Harcourt Brace.

"Klanwatch." 1998. *Southern Poverty Law Center, Internet.* July.

Kressel, Neil J. 1996. *Mass Hate: The Global Rise of Genocide and Terror.* New York: Plenum Press.

Kupperman, Robert H. 1985. "Terrorism and Public Policy: Domestic Impacts, International Threats." In *American Violence and Public Policy,* ed. Lynn A. Curtis. New Haven: Yale.

Lambert, Mary and Daniel Yurman. 1995. "Civil War Predicted in Idaho," *Western Lands Gopher Service.* [Internet/Alternet], 12, 15 March.

Larson, Erik, "Unrest in the West," *Time* 146 (17), 23 October 1995, 52-66.

Laqueur, Walter. 1987. *The Age of Terrorism.* Boston: Little, Brown and Company.

Leuchtenburg, William E. 1967. *The Perils of Prosperity: 1914–1932.* 12th ed. Chicago: The University of Chicago Press.

Leung, Rebecca. 1998. "Hate Crimes in America." *ABCNEWS.com.* 17 June.

Lipset, Seymour Martin, and Earl Raab. 1970. *The Politics of Unreason: Right-Wing Extremism in America, 1790–1970.* 1st ed. New York: Harper & Row.

Lindsey, Hal with C. C. Carlson. 1970. *The Late Great Planet Earth.* Grand Rapids, MI: Zondervan Publishing.

Macdonald, Andrew. (Pseud. for William L. Pierce.) 1985. *The Turner Diaries.* Arlington, VA: Nat'l. Vanguard books.

Macko, Steve. 1996. "Arizona Militia Group Arrested by Federal Authorities." *Emergency Net News Service [Internet]* 2 July. 2:184.

Mallinowski, Sean. 1998. "G-7 Takes Another Look at Terrorism," *CJ Europe Online.* [Internet] 23 February.

Marani, Mack, 1998. "The Michigan Militia: Political Engagement or Political Alienation." *Terrorism and Political Violence* 10 (4) 122-148.

Marsden, George M. 1980. *Fundamentalism and American Culture: The Shaping of Twentieth Century Evangelicalism, 1870-1925.* New York: Oxford University Press.

McClelland, Susan. 1999. "Straight, but with an Edge." *Maclean's,* 17 May.

McFeatters, Ann. 1999. "Polling Shows U.S. Optimism Fades." *Idaho State Journal.* 11 May. A-4.

McCulloch, Greg. 1996. *Legi-Slate* News Service bulletin. 17 April.

McQuillan, Laurence. 1998. "U.S. Says Attacks Aimed at Stopping New Bombings." *Reuters, Internet,* 20 August.

McGuckin, Frank. Editor. 1997. *Terrorism in the United States.* New York: H. W. Wilson. Co.

Melton, J. Gordon. 1978. *Encyclopedia of American Religions,* 2 volumes. Wilmington, NC: McGrath Publishing Co.

Militia of Montana Homepage. 1997. 7 May.

———. 1999. 1 April.

Millar, Robert G. 1998. "What the Press Does Not Say about Elohim City." *Right of Israel Online,* 30 July.

Milwaukee Journal Sentinel. 1999. [AP/*Washington Post* sources]. 5 July.

Minneapolis Star Tribune. 1998. "3 Whites Charged with Murder in Black Man's Dragging Death." 7 July.

———. 2000. "U.S. Urged to Get Tough on Terrorism." 4 June.

Monroe, Charles. "Addressing Terrorism in the United States," *Annals of the American Academy of Political and Social Science,* Vol. 463. September 1982.

Murray, Robert K. 1964. *Red Scare: A Study in National Hysteria 1919–1920.* 5th ed. New York: McGraw-Hill.

Netanyahu, Benjamin. 1995. *Fighting Terrorism: How Democracies Can Defeat Domestic and International Terrorism.* New York: Farrar Straus Giroux.

New Book of Knowledge, Volume 12. 1993.

New Lexicon Webster's Dictionary, Encyclopedic Edition, vol. 2. 1992. Danbury, CT: Lexicon Public Inc.

O'Callaghan, John. 1998. "Tanzanian Suspects Freed as Bomb Probe Continues." *Reuters, Internet,* 15 August.

O'Connor, Karen and Larry J. Sabato. 1995. *American Government: Roots and Reform,* 2nd ed. Boston: Allyn and Bacon.

Office for Victims of Crime Resource Center. 2000. *Responding to Terrorism Victims: Oklahoma City and Beyond,* Chapter VI: Legal Issues Pertaining to Victims of Terrorism [www.ojpusdog.gov/ovc/infors/respterrorism/chap6.html] October.

Office of the White House Press Secretary. 1996. "Counterterrorism." 20 April.

Painter, Brian. 1995. "Co-Workers Experienced Blast Close-up." *Daily Oklahoman* 19 May.

Peck, M. Scott. 1978. *The Road Less Traveled.* New York: Simon and Shuster.

Peck, M. Scott. 1998. *People of the Lie.* New York: Simon and Shuster.

Peters, Pete. 1998. "Armed and Dangerous—with Faith, Hope and Love." *Scriptures for America: Worldwide, online* 4 (1997), 21 February.

Phillips, Andrew. 1999. "Lessons of Littleton." *Maclean's.* 3 May.

Pierce, William. 1995. "Oklahoma City Bombing and America's Future," [Internet], 29 April.

Plano, Jack C. and Milton Greenberg, editors. 1993. *The American Political Dictionary,* 9th ed. New York: Harcourt Brace Jovanovich.

Portzline, Donnell B. 1965. "William Dudley Pelley and the Silver Shirt Legion of America." Ph.D. dissertation. Ball State University.

"Prominent Patriots List." 1998. *Southern Poverty Law Center Militia Task Force, Internet,* 22 July.

"Race Riot." 1997. *Maclean's,* 17 February.

Reuters, Internet. 1998. "Five Freemen Convicted." 1 April.

———. 1998. "Islamic Group Claims Anti-U.S. Attacks, Vows More." 8 August.

———. 1998. "Klan Ordered to Pay Torched Black Church." 25 July.

Riley, Kevin Jack and Bruce Hoffman. 1995. *Domestic Terrorism: A National Assessment of State and Local Preparedness.* Santa Monica, CA: Rand Corporation.

Robertson, Pat. 1990. *The New Millennium.* Dallas: Word Publications.

Schonbach, Morris. 1985. "Native American Fascism during the 1930s and 1940s." Ph.D. Dissertation. University of California Los Angeles.

Sears, David O. and Jack Citrin. 1986. "Tax Revolt: Proposition 13 in California and Its Aftermath." In *Bureaucratic Power in National Policy Making,* 4th ed. Ed. Francis E. Rourke. Boston: Little, Brown and Co.

Simon, Herbert. 1976. *Administrative Behavior,* 3rd ed. New York: Macmillan.

Smith, Brent L. 1994. *Terrorism in America: Pipe Bombs and Pipe Dreams.* Albany: State University of New York Press.

Smolowe, Jill, "Enemies of the State," *Time* 145 (19), 8 May 1995, 58-69.

Southern Poverty Law Center. *Intelligence Project Internet.* 17 May 2001.

Southern Poverty Law Center. *Intelligence Report, Internet.* Winter 1998.

Spitz, David. 1965. *Patterns of Anti-Democratic Thought,* rev. ed. New York: Free Press.

Stalking the Wild Taboo—Latest news, Internet. 1996. "1996 *AR* Conference a Huge Success." [www.amren.com/conf.96htm] May.

Sterling, Claire. 1981. *The Terror Network: The Secret War of International Terrorism.* New York: Holt, Rinehart and Wilson.

Stern, Kenneth S. 1997. *A Force Upon the Plain: The American Militia Movement and the Politics of Hate.* Norman: University of Oklahoma Press.

Stickney, Brandon M. 1996. *All-American Monster: The Unauthorized Biography of Timothy McVeigh.* Amherst, New York: Prometheus Books.

Strauss, William and Neil Howe. 1997. *The Fourth Turning: An American Prophecy.* New York: Broadway Books.

Subcommittee on Civil and Constitutional Rights on the Committee on the Judiciary, First Session. 1981. "Report on Domestic and International Terrorism." Washington, D.C.: U.S. Government Printing Office. April.

Tabor, James D. And Eugene V. Gallagher. 1995. *Why Waco? Cults and the Battle for Religious Freedom in America.* Berkley: University of California Press.

Taylor, Jared. 1996. "Race and Nation: A Speech at the 1996 *AR* Conference." [Internet], May. Louisville, KY.

Tilove, Jonathan. 1998. "The Coming White Minority." *Minneapolis Star Tribune* [Newhouse News Service]. 13 July.

Times of India–online. 2001. [www.times of india.com] 17 February.

Toffler, Alvin and Heidi. 1993. *War and Anti-War: Survival at the Dawn of the 21st Century.* Boston: Little, Brown and Company.

Tulsa World. 1997. 25 July.

———. 1998. 13 May.

USA Today—Nation, Internet. 1998. "Race Killing in Texas Fuels Fear, Anger." July.

U.S. Commission on National Security/21st Century. 2000. *Phase III Report*, Executive Summary vii–xvii. [www.nssg.gov] 31 January.

U.S. Department of Justice, Federal Bureau of Investigation. 1958. *The Ku Klux Klan: Section 1—1865–1944*. Washington, D.C.

United States Department of Justice, Federal Bureau of Investigation. 1998. *Uniform Crime Reports: Hate Crime—1995* [Internet] 15 August.

United States Department of Justice, Federal Bureau of Investigation. 2000. CJ Info Services (online), "Hate Crime Statistics." 19 May.

United States Department of State. *1996 and 1997 Patterns of Global Terrorism.* Washington: [www.state.gov/www/global/terrorism.] 1996, 1997.

United States General Accounting Office. 1997. "Report to Congressional Requesters—Combating Terrorism," Internet/Terrorism Research Center. 5 December.

U.S. Department of State (Office of the Coordinator for Counterterrorism). 1995. "International Terrorism: American Hostages." 17 October.

U.S. Department of State (Office of the Coordinator for Counterterrorism). 1997. "Implementation of the 25 Recommendations from the Paris Ministerial." 11 December.

U.S. Department of State [Office of the coordinator for Counterterrorism]. 2001. *Report 2000—Year in Review.* April.

Vogel, Ed. 1997. "Militia Movement Figure Moves to Vegas." *Law Vegas Review–Journal Online.* 17 November.

Watson, Francis M. 1976. *Political Terrorism: The Threat and the Response.* New York: Robert B. Luce Co., Inc.

Webb, Gary. 1998. *Dark Alliance: The CIA, the Contras, and the Crack Cocaine Explosion.* New York: Seven Stories Press.

Webster's New Collegiate Dictionary. 1965. Springfield, MA: Merriam Co.

Wheeler, Eugene D. and S. Anthony Baron. 1994. *Violence in Our Schools, Hospitals and Public Places: A Prevention and Management Guide.* Ventura, CA: Pathfinder Publishing

White Nationalist Links, Internet. 1998. Update 11 February.

White Pride Worldwide [WPWW.com]. 1998. 14 August.

Whitworth, Damian. 1999. "Gloomy Tribal Craze That Was Born in Britain." *The Times* [London]. 22 April.

Wilkie, Curtis. 1999. "Duke Queried on Mailings, Invokes Fifth Amendment." *Boston Globe, Internet.* 21 May.

Wilson, James Q. 1986. "The Rise of the Bureaucratic State." In *Bureaucratic Power in National Policy Making,* 4th ed. Ed. Francis E. Rourke. Boston: Little, Brown and Co.

Wilson, J. Brent. 1994. "The United States' Response to International Terrorism," In *The Deadly Sin of Terrorism.* Ed. David A. Charters. Westport, CT: Greenwood Press.

Winona Daily News. 1997. 23 February.

———. 1999. 15 February.

WKBT–Channel 8. News at 10. "Covering Our World." 2001. 17 May.

Yang, John E. 1996. "House Votes to Remove Controversial Provisions from Anti-terrorism Bill." *Washington Post* [Internet-*Legi-Slate* article]. 14 March.

Yurman, Dan. 1996. "Idaho's Plutonium Landscape." *The Progressive Populist, Internet Edition.* January.

Zook, Matthew A. 1996. "The Unorganized Militia Network: Conspiracies, Computers, and Community." *Berkley Planning Journal* (11) [http://socrates.berkeley.edu/~zook/pubs/Militia[paper.html].

Special Collections

U.S. Congress. Senate. Foreign Relations Committee, 1959-1980. "Treaties." Series 2.2. Box 17.20. Frank Church Papers. Boise: Boise State University, Albertsons Library.

U.S. Congress. Senate. (Index) Select Committee on Intelligence Activities, 1966-1977 and 1978-1980. Series 2.6. Box 1. Frank Church Papers. Boise: Boise State University, Albertsons Library.

U.S. Congress. Senate. Campaigns. "1980 Senatorial Elections." Series 5.6. Box 2. Folder 6. Frank Church Papers. Boise: Boise State University, Albertsons Library.

U.S. Congress. Senate. Public Relations. "Radical Right." Series 7.5. Box 1. Folder 3. Frank Church Papers. Boise: Boise State University, Albertsons Library.

Index